Early praise for *Clojure Applied*

Starting your first Clojure job? Kicking off your first big open source Clojure project? This is the book you need to get started building Clojure projects. You may worry, "I don't know what I don't know." This book points you to the things you need to know.

➤ **Bridget Hillyer**
Software developer, LivingSocial

While other Clojure books enumerate the beautiful, pristine qualities derived from immutability and functional programming, this book is about getting your hands very dirty. *Clojure Applied* takes you step by step through the process of designing, writing, and shipping robust, high-performance production systems.

➤ **David Nolen**
Software developer, Cognitect

It's refreshing to see experts such as Ben and Alex distill their knowledge into a tome for the masses. *Clojure Applied* covers a myriad of subjects that perplexed me about Clojure on my own journey. I'm hopeful the book will short-circuit the journey for many.

➤ **Ryan Neufeld**
Software consultant, founder, Homegrown Labs

Clojure Applied is the book I wish I had when I started writing Clojure. This book is packed with advice and tips based on years of real-world experience. I learned something new on what seemed like every page. Buy this book and take your Clojure code to the next level.

➤ **Larry Staton, Jr.**
  Senior software engineer, Hendrick Automotive Group

I had a solid foundation and collection of recipes. When I was ready for the next level, *Clojure Applied* gave me application patterns and instructed me on how to apply them in an idiomatic way, quickly. *Clojure Applied* clearly articulates the voices of the authors of the language and libraries, teaching me to design applications in the way the language and its components were designed for.

➤ **Adam Hunter**
  Software development lead, TMA, Inc.

If you admire the design of the Clojure language and would like to learn how to apply the same principles to your own code, then this is the book for you.

➤ **David McNeil**
  Software developer, LonoCloud

Clojure Applied

From Practice to Practitioner

Ben Vandgrift
Alex Miller

The Pragmatic Bookshelf

Dallas, Texas • Raleigh, North Carolina

Our Pragmatic courses, workshops, and other products can help you and your team create better software and have more fun. For more information, as well as the latest Pragmatic titles, please visit us at *https://pragprog.com*.

The team that produced this book includes:

Jacquelyn Carter (editor)
Potomac Indexing, LLC (index)
Eileen Cohen (copyedit)
Dave Thomas (layout)
Janet Furlow (producer)
Ellie Callahan (support)

For international rights, please contact *rights@pragprog.com*.

Printed in the United States of America.
ISBN-13: 978-1-68050-074-5
Printed on acid-free paper.
Book version: P1.0—September 2015

Contents

Part II — Applications

Part III — Practices

Foreword

For most people, the process of learning Clojure proceeds in three stages. First are the fundamentals: when do I use parentheses and when do I use brackets? How is a vector different from a list? And what's the syntax for a function literal again?

The middle stage of learning Clojure is when you work out how it all fits together. How do I assemble all these first-class functions into working code? How do I turn laziness into an ally instead of a confusing adversary? And just how do I get anything done with data structures that I can't modify?

Once you have enough understanding of the language to be able to bootstrap from what you know to what you want to know, you enter the third and final stage of learning Clojure. This is when you explore the Clojure ecosystem of libraries and applications, using your new knowledge to work out what other people have built and how they went about building it. This is also when most people start making their own contributions. It's all fun, but the third stage is when the *serious* fun kicks in.

Given how minimal Clojure's syntax is, the first stage usually goes quickly and painlessly. The third stage generally takes quite a bit longer, but most people don't seem to notice since they're having such a good time. It's that middle phase that tends to be the challenge: you understand the basics but aren't quite sure what you do with them. For example, functional programming is a straightforward idea: you write your code as a series of functions that do nothing but take some arguments and produce a result. Getting the hang of actually writing functional programs—of assembling these little bits of algorithm into a working whole—is a much bigger challenge. The same is true of many of the other concepts embraced by Clojure: simple and easy to grasp, harder to assemble into a working whole. The middle stage of learning Clojure is when you really learn Clojure.

Clojure Applied is aimed squarely at the middle stage of learning Clojure. If you know how to write Clojure functions but still aren't 100 percent sure how you do this functional programming *thing*, this book can help you. If you know how to fill up all those persistent data structures with data, but you aren't sure where to go from there, this is the book for you. If you find yourself struggling with the issues of state and when and how it should change, keep reading. As the name suggests, *Clojure Applied* is about using Clojure to solve real problems and build real code—and get to the serious fun.

Most people find that once they learn Clojure it's hard to go back. Get used to Clojure's finely honed minimalism, its elegant and powerful approach to programming, and you wonder how you ever lived without it. As I say, there's no going back. But with this book, Alex and Ben have come back. They've come back for you. They've come back to be your guide, to help you through the middle stage of learning Clojure, the *after the basics but before mastery* part of the trip. Enjoy the ride.

Russ Olsen

Herndon, VA, April 1, 2015

Acknowledgments

This book wouldn't have been possible without the help of many people. They did their level best to make this book spectacular, and where it falls short, the fault is entirely ours.

We'd like to thank the staff at Pragmatic Bookshelf, our editor Jacquelyn Carter, managing editor Susannah Pfalzer, and the publishers Andy Hunt and Dave Thomas. Jackie provided us with excellent advice and dealt patiently with our often hectic schedules.

Thanks to Rich Hickey for creating our favorite programming language and for helping us think about good problems. Thanks to everyone at Cognitect for being great colleagues and supporting both Clojure and the book. Additionally, thanks to the Clojure community—you continually amaze us with your ideas and contributions.

Thanks to those who reviewed the book both on and off the record: Mario Aquino, Kevin Archie, Aaron Arnett, Stu Halloway, Bridget Hillyer, Adam Hunter, Ben Kamphaus, David McNeil, Andrew Mertz, Ryan Neufeld, Russ Olsen, Alex Stangl, and Larry Staton, Jr.

An especially heartfelt thanks to Russ Olsen for his excellent foreword, and for the many times he gave sound advice on how to sound as patient, encouraging, and friendly as he does by reflex alone.

Thank you to those who posted feedback through the discussion forums, errata page, and other online communities. A special thanks to Stig Brautaset, who contributed generously to the asynchronous shopping example in *Shopping with a Pack*, on page 75.

From Alex:

Thanks first to Ben, both for asking me to participate in this effort, and then for not kicking me out when I suggested substantial changes in direction.

Thanks to my daughter Ella for an unending stream of humorous faux book reviews and requests to read the book. Thanks to my son Truman for (mostly) not playing drums outside my office during writing time. Thanks to my son Beck for the reminder that there's always time to get shot by a NERF gun. Finally, the biggest thanks go to my wife Mary for her love and support despite far too many late nights of writing. It's all done now, I promise!

From Ben:

Thank you Alex, for sharing this journey with me, pushing the book in the right directions, and being a rock I could count on. You've helped make this work *much* better than I could've alone.

Thanks to many friends for constant encouragement, particularly Carl and Elaine. You two won't read this book, but you're the reason I thought I could write it.

Caffeinated thanks to Central Coffee[1] and Not Just Coffee,[2] where most of my writing got done.

Most of all, thank you to my wife Christina for her support, patience, occasional kicks in the shin, and for allowing me to continue working on the text while we planned our wedding. So oh oh.

---

1.   http://tinyurl.com/centralcoffee
2.   http://www.notjust.coffee/

Introduction

Taking a programming language out of the toy box and into the workplace can be a daunting prospect. If you haven't designed or developed a life-size application in Clojure before, you may not know where to begin, how to proceed, or what your day-to-day development process will look like. You're not alone, and we're here to help. We're going to show you how to take your Clojure practice to the professional level.

Clojure's focus on data, Lisp syntax, and functional leanings can empower you to write elegant applications. Learning to take full advantage of these facilities, though, is more than just syntax. Think about the game of chess.

Understanding how to play chess is more than understanding which pieces can move where. Broader concerns are involved: choosing an opening, pressuring and holding the center, the transition to the midgame, trapping your opponent's king. You can play the game the minute you understand the mechanics, but achieving any level of satisfying victory requires an understanding of the larger concepts.

Learning Clojure is no different. The syntax and behavior are only the first step toward proficiency. Understanding the language's principles and putting them into practice is the next step.

When you're new to any topic it helps to have strong guidelines with which to operate. Rules become practice, practice becomes habit, and habit becomes instinct. Before long, you'll have a nose for doing the right thing.

As you strengthen your practice, you'll know which rules can be bent and evolve your own personal style. You'll eventually outgrow the techniques we present, but by then—we hope!—you'll look fondly back at this text as one of your stepping stones to mastery.

Putting Clojure to Work

All Clojure applications build upon a foundation of immutable values. Immutability is present not just for simple scalar values but also for composite values like lists, vectors, maps, and sets. The axiom of immutability underlies our approach to data transformation, state, concurrency, and even API design.

In this book, you'll learn to build Clojure applications from bottom to top, then how to take those systems to production. This process starts from simple concepts and builds larger units of code until the application has full functionality.

We'll start by looking at how to model a problem domain with domain entities and relationships. You'll learn how to choose the best data structure to use when collecting values and entities in your domain, including some lesser-known and more-specialized options. If none of the available collections is sufficient, you'll even learn how to build your own custom collection that can work with the existing Clojure core library.

Once you have your data representation, you need to consider how to transform both your entities and collections. For this, you can rely primarily on the tools of functional programming. Most of the functions you'll create in a Clojure program are pure: they transform one immutable value (whether it's an entity, collection, sequence, or tree) to another immutable value without side effects. This pairing of immutable values and pure functions makes your code easy to understand, easy to test, and immune to many of the problems caused by unmanaged mutability.

Building Applications

Once we've developed a representation of our data and the basic operations upon it, we need to consider how to build up from there into larger structures that compose an application. This will require things like state, concurrency, and components.

The combination of immutable values and pure functions provides exactly the foundation we need to create and maintain state. In Clojure, state is the current value referenced by an identity. State changes happen when an update function transforms the current value to a new value. Clojure has several stateful reference types that can establish a shared identity. You'll learn how to select the best reference type for your needs.

Although this state model is simple, it's the secret to Clojure's suitability for writing concurrent programs. When you can rely on immutable values and a simple model for state changes, it becomes much easier to use concurrency to scale up your processing. You'll learn how to leverage Clojure concurrency techniques for both doing work in the background and processing data in parallel.

We then need to move to bigger units of code to accomplish bigger goals. You'll learn how to leverage namespaces to organize code and how to design components. Components expose functionality through an API and can contain state and manage concurrency. Components can even aggregate other components and act as application subsystems.

Finally, it's time to assemble the whole application by gluing together components. You'll learn how to load your system configuration, instantiate components, connect those components, and provide entry points for the application as a whole.

This process of building systems from bottom to top is logical, but it's unlikely that you'll follow it in linear order in every real application. You may start at the bottom developing a data model, but you may also start at the top, determining how a system will be broken up into subsystems or components, and how those components are connected. Most likely you'll bounce back and forth and do both!

Both directions of work allow us to gain a greater understanding of the problem. Only an iterative process combining information from both will allow the shape of the final solution to emerge. Nevertheless, you should expect that the end application will contain the pieces we discussed in the preceding text when you get to the end.

From Build to Deploy

After you've seen an overview of how to build a Clojure application, you'll need to consider other concerns, such as testing, integration, and deployment.

When you look into testing Clojure code, you'll find that Clojure developers lean away from example-based unit testing and more toward other approaches such as interactive development in the REPL and model- or property-oriented approaches that can survey a wider range of inputs for correctness. This approach provides more coverage in less time and creates tests that are easier to maintain over time. However, it's a shift in thinking, and some practice is required to yield the greatest benefits.

You may also need to connect your Clojure-based application to other systems, either by integrating a web or other user interface, exposing an API service, or consuming external APIs. The Clojure approach to these problems, unsurprisingly, treats data (and the transmission of data over wires) with importance. You'll learn about some of the available options and which ones to use in different situations to maximize performance or extensibility.

Finally, you need to deploy your application to cloud-based containers. We'll look at some of the most popular choices and how to choose among them.

About This Book

This book is a bridge from introductory material to solving real problems with Clojure, providing a guide to thinking about problems in ways that are harmonious with the tools provided.

Who This Book Is For

You should be familiar with Clojure's basic concepts and syntax to read this book. You'll learn to connect the pieces you already know to support the larger goal of building great applications.

How to Read This Book

Parts 1 and 2 should be read in order, because each chapter builds on previous topics. It's a narrative, not a reference. Part 3 can be read in any order. Each chapter in Part 3 is self-contained but may depend at times on content discussed in Parts 1 and 2.

Code and Notation

Whether in a code block or embedded in text, code uses the following font:

```
(println "Hello!")
```

For commands to be typed in a REPL, the namespace is shown (in this case, user) and a slightly different highlighting scheme used. Any output relevant to the evaluated statement is in code font immediately below the executed code:

```
user=> (println "Hello!")
Hello!
```

The location of source code that can be found in the accompanying source bundle precedes the code:

```
cljapplied/src/preface.clj
(+ 5 4 3 2 1)
```

In several instances we add indentation (as you might see in Clojure source) to output, for clarity:

```
user=> (current-customer)
#Customer{:cname "Danny Tanner",
          :email "danny@fullhouse.example.com",
          :membership-number 28374}
```

In other instances, we use a nonstandard (but useful) convention to denote code that has been elided for brevity. Three commas ,,, mark a section of code that's been removed for brevity. You may see this type of ellipsis referred to as the *Fogus comma*.[1]

Online Resources

The code examples we use are available online at the Pragmatic Bookshelf website.[2] A community forum is also available there for discussion, questions, and submitting any errata you find.

To get the most out of the examples, you'll want to install Clojure. A number of good online resources[3] are available, but the easiest way to get Clojure on your system is to install Leiningen.[4]

Alex Miller and Ben Vandgrift

August 2015

---

1. http://blog.fogus.me/2013/09/04/a-ha-ha-ha-aah/
2. https://pragprog.com/book/vmclojeco/clojure-applied
3. http://ben.vandgrift.com/2014/03/14/clojure-getting-started.html
4. http://leiningen.org/

Part I

Foundations

Clojure applications are based on two fundamental tools: immutable values and pure functions. You'll learn how to define the domain model in terms of immutable values, and how to transform that model using transformation functions.

## CHAPTER 1

Model Your Domain

Data is the bedrock of our programs. It's what we build everything else on, so it's the first thing we consider when developing an application. Clojure makes data immutable and stable while exposing it for generic access. This makes code simpler, easier to reason about, and more concise.

Clojure has a great set of tools for representing any domain as data, but sometimes it's not clear how to get from a block of stone to a finished sculpture. We're going to show you how to apply a range of techniques—from basic to advanced—for creating the best structure for your data.

Pick up your chisels—we've got some data sculpting to do!

Modeling Entities

Any programming effort starts with a problem we want to solve. The first task we face is how to model the domain of the problem to express our solution. The decisions we make will affect how we interact with external systems as well as the algorithms and performance of our application. We'll start by considering how we should represent domain entities in Clojure.

In Clojure, we use either *maps* or *records* to represent domain entities. Maps are generic collections of key-value pairs, whereas records construct a type with predefined structure for well-known fields.

We're going to look at a number of considerations involved in choosing between maps and records based on expected usage patterns and performance needs. But let's start by reviewing how we use maps and records to model entities.

Maps

Maps have no predefined structure and few constraints, yielding great flexibility. Maps are a collection of key-value pairs that allow values to be looked up by key in *effectively constant* time. To use a map as an entity, we specify attribute names as keys, typically as keywords.

Effectively Constant Time

Maps, vectors, and sets are implemented in Clojure by Hash Array Mapped Tries using a 32-way branching factor. Lookups are based on tree traversal, which has time complexity $O(\log n)$. However, these Clojure data structures use a 32-way branching factor, so the actual lookup time is $O(\log_{32} n)$. Practically speaking, most maps require no more than two to three levels, and a map with a billion entries requires only six. Because this function grows so slowly we call lookups on these data structures *effectively constant*.

Suppose we've been tasked with creating a program to simulate the solar system. In our program we'll likely need entities to represent the sun, the planets, their moons, and perhaps other objects of note. Let's start with thinking about how to model Earth as an entity. Earth, as a planet, has a number of attributes that might be of interest in our simulation.

In Clojure, the simplest way to model an entity with a set of attributes is to use a Clojure map:

cljapplied/src/ch1/modeling.clj
```
(def earth {:name       "Earth"
            :moons      1
            :volume     1.08321e12 ;; km^3
            :mass       5.97219e24 ;; kg
            :aphelion   152098232  ;; km, farthest from sun
            :perihelion 147098290  ;; km, closest to sun
            })
```

As you'll see in later chapters, it's often useful to have an entity type that can be used to drive dynamic behavior. For example, we may want to find only the set of solar system entities that are planets. We can extend our example slightly by including an extra :type attribute to mark the entity:

cljapplied/src/ch1/modeling.clj
```
(def earth {:name       "Earth"
            :moons      1
            :volume     1.08321e12 ;; km^3
            :mass       5.97219e24 ;; kg
            :aphelion   152098232  ;; km, farthest from sun
            :perihelion 147098290  ;; km, closest to sun
            :type       :Planet    ;; entity type
            })
```

We now have a planet instance and even a usable entity type, but we didn't capture this structure (specifically the field names) in a way that's useful to other developers on our team.

Clojure *records* were designed for this purpose.

Records

Records provide some class-like features —well-known fields and constructors —to support domain entities. Records are created with a type name and fields:

cljapplied/src/ch1/modeling.clj
```
(defrecord Planet [name
                   moons
                   volume      ;; km^3
                   mass        ;; kg
                   aphelion    ;; km, farthest from sun
                   perihelion  ;; km, closest to sun
                   ])
```

Once the record structure is defined, we can use it to create many instances of the record with the same well-known fields. All instances of this record will have an observable type of Planet (in the namespace where we created it).

The fields of a defrecord are shared by all instances of a domain entity. In addition, two factory functions are automatically created to assist in creating new instances. For the Planet record, there will be a *positional factory function* (->Planet) that expects a value for each attribute in the order specified by defrecord and a *map factory function* (map->Planet) that expects a map with keyed values:

cljapplied/src/ch1/modeling.clj
```
;; Positional factory function
(def earth
     (->Planet "Earth" 1 1.08321e12 5.97219e24 152098232 147098290))

;; Map factory function
(def earth
     (map->Planet {:name       "Earth"
                   :moons      1
                   :volume     1.08321e12
                   :mass       5.97219e24
                   :aphelion   152098232
                   :perihelion 147098290}))
```

The positional factory function is more concise but requires all attributes to be included in the specified order, so callers are more likely to break if the record is changed. The map factory function allows the omission of optional attributes, provides more description, and continues to work even if new attributes are added to the record.

Deciding Between Maps and Records

Maps and records both use the standard map collection functions for access and modification, but most of the time records are a better choice for domain entities. Records leverage features of the host platform—the Java Virtual Machine (JVM)—to provide better performance in several ways. Records define their type by creating a Java class with a field for each attribute. A record can thus take primitive type hints in its field definition and will create primitive fields in the underlying Java class, which provides a more efficient representation and faster arithmetic for numbers. The underlying Java class also provides a place to implement Java interfaces and Clojure protocols, placing behavior directly on the record and providing the fastest possible function dispatch for those cases.

Given that records give you well-known fields, a type, factory functions, and better performance, they should be your first choice for domain entities. Why might we use maps instead?

One specific case for which you should strongly consider maps is in public-facing APIs, whether they're expected to be consumed by Java or by Clojure. In an API, it's important to minimize the constraints on our callers. Requiring them to create instances of our record classes causes some of the details of those classes to be effectively public as well. In this case, maps with a well-known set of keys commit to less and are a simpler and better choice.

Don't fret about making the wrong choice between maps and records! Records effectively *are* maps in all important ways. Both maps and records present the same interface—you simply ask for an attribute value by key using functions like get. So it's easy to use records internally but only commit to the map aspects of records when returning entities from an API. The two main places you're likely to see differences are in construction and dynamic behavior based on type.

In addition to the factory functions provided by defrecord, it can be useful to define functions that provide more flexibility when you create entities. We'll address these in more detail next.

Constructing Entities

Once you've defined an entity's structure, you need to build functions that populate that structure. Most of the time, you populate your entities using defrecord's positional and map factory functions, or the core library functions to create maps (like {}, hash-map, and zipmap).

However, some common situations deserve a bit more consideration. One of the most common situations is the case of entities with optional values. Clojure can deal with this in a number of ways, and we'll look at some of the most common. We'll also look at constructors that create derived values or have side effects.

On Terms and Naming

We use the term *factory function* to specifically describe the functions created automatically by defrecord and *constructor* to refer to any other function that constructs new entity instances. However, be aware that these terms are often used interchangeably in the Clojure community and may have different connotations in other language communities.

It's useful to have a naming convention for constructor functions across your project. The Clojure community has no standard naming convention for constructors, but some of the most common constructor prefixes used are new-, make-, and map->. We'll primarily use make- but feel free to adopt your own convention—just use it consistently.

First we'll consider how to deal with optional arguments.

Constructing with Options

Use of optional arguments can give your constructors flexibility. If you're expecting to build entities in a variety of ways, optional arguments can help.

We can include optional arguments in the definition of a function by adding & opts to the arguments vector:

```
(defn fn-with-opts [f1 f2 & opts] ,,, )
```

Of course, opts can be named whatever you like. Optional arguments passed to the function are collected into a sequence and bound to opts within the function body.

Positional Destructuring

When defining constructors with optional arguments, you can use destructuring[1] for clarity:

```
(defn make-entity [f1 f2 & [f3 f4]] ,,, )
```

---

1. http://clojure.org/special_forms

This allows any number of optional arguments, binding f3 and f4 based on their position. Clojure's destructuring capabilities can vastly improve your quality of life as a developer. Any code in which you find yourself making frequent use of positional functions like first, second, or nth can typically be more simply written with destructuring.

You can use this technique to define a constructor function that takes zero or more fields, prioritized by dependency. Let's look at a snippet concerned with manipulating currency. Along with methods for adding currency (+$) and multiplying sums by a number (*$), we want a Money entity that encapsulates a money value in a particular currency.

In *Patterns of Enterprise Application Architecture [Fow03]*, Martin Fowler describes a representation of monetary values that avoids many of the pitfalls of using a floating-point number, while abstracting away issues of currency. Let's build a Money value object in Clojure. We start with the records to model the values:

cljapplied/src/ch1/money.clj
```
(ns ch1.money)

(declare validate-same-currency)

(defrecord Currency [divisor sym desc])

(defrecord Money [amount ^Currency currency]
  java.lang.Comparable
    (compareTo [m1 m2]
      (validate-same-currency m1 m2)
      (compare (:amount m1) (:amount m2))))

(def currencies {:usd (->Currency 100 "USD" "US Dollars")
                 :eur (->Currency 100 "EUR" "Euro")})
```

We also need functions for adding, comparing, multiplying, and other operations:

cljapplied/src/ch1/money.clj
```
(defn- validate-same-currency
  [m1 m2]
  (or (= (:currency m1) (:currency m2))
      (throw
        (ex-info "Currencies do not match."
          {:m1 m1 :m2 m2}))))

(defn =$
  ([m1] true)
  ([m1 m2] (zero? (.compareTo m1 m2))))
```

```
  ([m1 m2 & monies]
    (every? zero? (map #(.compareTo m1 %) (conj monies m2)))))

(defn +$
  ([m1] m1)
  ([m1 m2]
    (validate-same-currency m1 m2)
    (->Money (+ (:amount m1) (:amount m2)) (:currency m1)))
  ([m1 m2 & monies]
    (reduce +$ m1 (conj monies m2))))

(defn *$ [m n] (->Money (* n (:amount m)) (:currency m)))
```

Now let's build a flexible Money constructor that includes default values:

cljapplied/src/ch1/money.clj
```
(defn make-money
  ([] (make-money 0))
  ([amount] (make-money amount :usd))
  ([amount currency] (->Money amount currency)))
```

Now, from the REPL, we can call make-money in a number of ways:

```
(make-money)
;;-> #money.Money{:amount 0,
;;               :currency #money.Currency{:divisor 100,
;;                                         :sym "USD",
;;                                         :desc "US Dollars"}}

(make-money 1)
;;-> #money.Money{:amount 1,
;;               :currency #money.Currency{:divisor 100,
;;                                         :sym "USD",
;;                                         :desc "US Dollars"}}

(make-money 5 (:eur currencies))
;;-> #money.Money{:amount 5,
;;               :currency #money.Currency{:divisor 100,
;;                                         :sym "EUR",
;;                                         :desc "Euro"}}
```

In the function body, values more likely to be needed are placed earlier in the argument list.

Map Destructuring

Often, though, it's useful to accept optional arguments in any order. In this case, accepting a map of options that can be destructured is one simple solution:

```
(defn make-entity [f1 f2 {:keys [f3 f4] :as opts}] ,,, )
```

For example, consider extending our space simulation to also include data about the Apollo missions. These missions varied as to whether they were manned, had a lunar module, and so on. We can accept all of these options by destructuring a single map of options:

cljapplied/src/ch1/apollo.clj
```clojure
(defn make-mission
  [name system launched manned? opts]
  (let [{:keys [cm-name ;; command module
                lm-name ;; lunar module
                orbits
                evas]} opts]
    ,,, ))

(def apollo-4
  (make-mission "Apollo 4"
                "Saturn V"
                #inst "1967-11-09T12:00:01-00:00"
                false
                {:orbits 3}))
```

A set of default values can be provided by merging the incoming opts map with a map of defaults:

cljapplied/src/ch1/apollo.clj
```clojure
(def mission-defaults {:orbits 0, :evas 0})

(defn make-mission
  [name system launched manned? opts]
  (let [{:keys [cm-name ;; command module
                lm-name ;; lunar module
                orbits
                evas]} (merge mission-defaults opts)]
    ,,, ))
```

The merge works left-to-right with successive entries replacing prior ones, so in this example the mission-defaults come first and are then overridden by the opts if they were passed.

Another common way to accept optional arguments is to destructure the varargs sequence as a map (note the extra &):

cljapplied/src/ch1/apollo.clj
```clojure
(defn make-mission
  [name system launched manned? & opts]
  (let [{:keys [cm-name ;; command module
                lm-name ;; lunar module
                orbits
                evas]} opts]
    ,,, ))
```

```
(def apollo-4 (make-mission "Apollo 4"
                            "Saturn V"
                            #inst "1967-11-09T12:00:01-00:00"
                            false
                            :orbits 3))

(def apollo-11 (make-mission "Apollo 11"
                             "Saturn V"
                             #inst "1969-07-16T13:32:00-00:00" true
                             :cm-name "Columbia"
                             :lm-name "Eagle"
                             :orbits 30
                             :evas 1))
```

In both of these cases, you may find it useful to provide default values for some of the options. This can be done by using :or destructuring to provide the defaults:

cljapplied/src/ch1/apollo.clj
```
(defn make-mission
  [name system launched manned? & opts]
  (let [{:keys [cm-name ;; command module
                lm-name ;; lunar module
                orbits
                evas]
         :or {orbits 0, evas 0}} opts]    ;; default to 0
    ,,, ))

(def apollo-4 (make-mission "Apollo 4"
                "Saturn V"
                #inst "1967-11-09T12:00:01-00:00"
                false
                :orbits 3))
```

This example provides a default value of 0 for the evas and orbits keys. Other default values could be added to the :or map as well.

Constructor Calculations

So far, we've shown constructors as a way to populate an entity with options. A constructor can also include calculations required to create an entity from derived values. To demonstrate this, let's reconsider the Planet entity we defined on page 5:

```
(defrecord Planet [name moons volume
                   mass aphelion perihelion])
```

This definition would be sufficient for a planetary catalog. However, if we're writing an application that models the orbital mechanics of planets around a central star, we might need to know a little more about the planet's orbit. Don't worry about understanding the mathematics behind orbital mechanics —you're not here to learn astrophysics.

Let's assume that the information we receive to construct our planet entity includes an eccentricity vector. Using that vector, let's add the planet's orbital eccentricity (the amount the orbit deviates from a perfect circle) to our entity:

cljapplied/src/ch1/apollo.clj
```
(defn euclidean-norm [ecc-vector] ,,,)

(defrecord Planet
  [name moons volume mass aphelion perihelion orbital-eccentricity])

(defn make-planet
  "Make a planet from field values and an eccentricity vector"
  [name moons volume mass aphelion perhelion ecc-vector]
  (->Planet
    name moons volume mass aphelion perhelion
    (euclidean-norm ecc-vector)))
```

To get from an eccentricity vector to the orbital eccentricity, we apply the euclidean-norm to that vector. We use the result to call the record's positional factory function (->Planet).

Constructors with Side Effects

Sometimes the initialization of an entity includes unavoidable side effects, such as I/O. Using a constructor for this purpose isolates those side effects from the rest of the code.

For example, consider our solar system simulation and the need to load an image file for use as a PlanetImage in our simulation:

cljapplied/src/ch1/image.clj
```
(ns ch1.image
  (:require [clojure.java.io :as io])
  (:import [javax.imageio ImageIO]
           [java.awt.image BufferedImage]))

(defrecord PlanetImage [src ^BufferedImage contents])

(defn make-planet-image
  "Make a PlanetImage; may throw IOException"
  [src]
  (with-open [img (ImageIO/read (io/input-stream src))]
    (->PlanetImage src img)))
```

Rendering an image requires the BufferedImage captured in contents. By consolidating this into the constructor, we effectively automate the I/O we know we'll require. Using side effects in this way often adds complexity, however. In this example, we must be prepared to deal with an IOException thrown by either ImageIO/read or input-stream whenever we construct a PlanetImage.

Constructor Functions and Java Interop

Constructor functions are useful when one of your domain entities is imported from Java. Java classes often have many constructors for a variety of types—some of which have the same arity—and don't always do exactly what you want. A constructor function can provide a clean API to work with in these cases and keeps the interop and type hinting out of your way.

Default Entities

Finally, sometimes we want to create an entity representing a zero quantity or an empty container. You could create a function to construct a single entity in its default state. For example, new-money creates a Money instance with a value of $0.00 usd:

```
(defn new-money
  "$0.00 usd"
  []
  (->Money 0 :usd))
```

Remember, though, that Clojure uses immutable values. If your default entity function is always returning the same value, it's more efficient to declare it as a zero-dollars value rather than as a function:

```
(def zero-dollars (->Money 0 :usd))
```

Thinking in this way goes with the flow of Clojure's immutability and can clean up your code.

Now that you know many ways to model and construct entities, let's consider how we can start to combine them with relationships.

Modeling Relationships

Entities by themselves aren't much use. Most models will need to connect entities of different types to create relationships in the data, like the foreign keys in a SQL database.

An entity can use three main techniques to refer to another entity: nesting, identifiers, and stateful references. All of these techniques have analogues in other languages (and databases), but Clojure users prioritize the use of these techniques differently than in other languages. Languages like Java rely heavily on stateful references from one mutable object to another. Clojure users use the nesting and identifier techniques first and fall back to stateful references only in special cases.

Nesting simply means including another entity directly under a parent entity. Nesting is an easy choice when the nested entity is part of the parent entity and will follow its life cycle.

Let's consider a real example. If we're building a recipe-manager application, we obviously need to model a recipe:

cljapplied/src/ch1/recipe.clj
```
(defrecord Recipe
  [name        ;; string
   author      ;; recipe creator
   description ;; string
   ingredients ;; list of ingredients
   steps       ;; sequence of string
   servings    ;; number of servings
   ])
```

We won't cover all the details of this until later. Focus for now on the recipe's author field. We'll keep our author model simple for the moment:

cljapplied/src/ch1/recipe.clj
```
(defrecord Person
  [fname ;; first name
   lname ;; last name
   ])
```

Now let's consider the options we have for connecting Recipe and Person instances. If we're interested in making the Recipe the centerpiece of our application and consider authors to be merely descriptive information about the recipe, we can nest the person underneath the recipe:

cljapplied/src/ch1/recipe.clj
```
(def toast
  (->Recipe
    "Toast"
    (->Person "Alex" "Miller") ;; nested
    "Crispy bread"
    ["Slice of bread"]
    ["Toast bread in toaster"]
    1))
```

However, another version of our application might consider the authors to be of more importance. Users might expect that updating a person's information in one recipe will update that information in all the recipes. In that case, we might want to model the Person as the primary entity and have the person nest a list of Recipes he or she has authored.

Or you might want both Person and Recipe to be top-level entities that can each be updated in a single place. For example, a Recipe might have multiple authors. In this case, we may not want to rely on nesting at instead refer to an entity by a well-known *identifier*. An identifier is a simple value (usually a keyword, string, or number) that refers to an entity defined elsewhere. Let's rework our data model to allow recipes and authors to be managed indepedently:

```
cljapplied/src/ch1/recipe.clj
(def people
  {"p1" (->Person "Alex" "Miller")})

(def recipes
  {"r1" (->Recipe
          "Toast"
          "p1" ;; Person id
          "Crispy bread"
          ["Slice of bread"]
          ["Toast bread in toaster"]
          1)})
```

In this example we maintain two maps (people and recipes) that index entities by identifier. When a Recipe needs to refer to a Person as an author, it uses the Person's identifier instead of nesting the entity directly. Now we can find and modify both Person and Recipe entities independently.

It's almost always a good idea to generate identifiers programmatically (your database often generates them for you) and not allow the user to choose or edit the identifier. This gives you the most freedom to change your modeling strategy later without affecting users.

When you want to refer to another entity and allow that relationship to change over time, use a stateful reference. Clojure provides several state constructs that we'll examine in much more detail in Chapter 4, *State, Identity, and Change*, on page 63.

The *stateful reference* technique is the closest to the object-oriented practice of creating a graph of objects. However, in Clojure it's rare to use state inside the data model and much more common to use nesting or identifiers and create state only around large chunks of application data.

Next we'll look at one way to keep your entities valid as your project evolves.

Validating Entities

Once we have our domain model, we need a way to validate whether our data conforms to it. Clojure's dynamic types give us great power and flexibility but also enforce fewer constraints by default. Data validation is an area in which Clojure gives us choices about when, where, and how much validation we want to provide. In areas where data is created by our code, we may want to do little or no validation, whereas we may need significant validation when accepting data from external sources.

A number of external libraries exist to provide data description and validation support. We'll focus on Prismatic's Schema[2] library, but you may also want to look at core.typed,[3] clj-schema,[4] Strucjure,[5] or seqex.[6]

The Prismatic Schema library describes type metadata as data, automates descriptions, and validates data at runtime against that metadata. To add the Schema library to a project, add the following dependency in Leiningen:

cljapplied/project.clj

```
[prismatic/schema "0.4.3"]
```

Let's look at how to describe some data with Schema in the context of our recipe-manager application. This time we'll work out the details of the ingredients in the recipe:

cljapplied/src/ch1/validate.clj

```
(defrecord Recipe
  [name          ;; string
   description   ;; string
   ingredients   ;; sequence of Ingredient
   steps         ;; sequence of string
   servings      ;; number of servings
   ])

(defrecord Ingredient
  [name      ;; string
   quantity  ;; amount
   unit      ;; keyword
   ])
```

2.   https://github.com/prismatic/schema
3.   https://github.com/clojure/core.typed
4.   https://github.com/runa-dev/clj-schema
5.   https://github.com/jamii/strucjure
6.   https://github.com/jclaggett/seqex

We've added comments to these records to help our colleagues (and maybe ourselves a few months down the line) understand what we expect. A particular instance of a recipe might look like this:

```
cljapplied/src/ch1/validate.clj
(def spaghetti-tacos
  (map->Recipe
    {:name "Spaghetti tacos"
     :description "It's spaghetti... in a taco."
     :ingredients [(->Ingredient "Spaghetti" 1 :lb)
                   (->Ingredient "Spaghetti sauce" 16 :oz)
                   (->Ingredient "Taco shell" 12 :shell)]
     :steps ["Cook spaghetti according to box."
             "Heat spaghetti sauce until warm."
             "Mix spaghetti and sauce."
             "Put spaghetti in taco shells and serve."]
     :servings 4}))
```

Let's use Schema to describe our recipes instead. Schema has its own version of defrecord that adds the ability to specify a schema for values of each field (in addition to the normal effects of defrecord). Schema is specified after the :-, which is a special keyword that Schema uses as a syntactic marker.

First, pull in the Schema namespace:

```
cljapplied/src/ch1/validate.clj
(ns ch1.validate
  (:require [schema.core :as s]))
```

Then, redefine the records using the Schema version of defrecord:

```
cljapplied/src/ch1/validate.clj
(s/defrecord Ingredient
  [name     :- s/Str
   quantity :- s/Int
   unit     :- s/Keyword])

(s/defrecord Recipe
  [name        :- s/Str
   description :- s/Str
   ingredients :- [Ingredient]
   steps       :- [s/Str]
   servings    :- s/Int])
```

Normal type hints and class names (like String) are valid schema descriptions, but we've used the built-in schemas like s/Str instead. These schemas are portable and yield the proper check in both Clojure and ClojureScript. The schema for ingredients is a sequence of items of type Ingredient. The steps field is a sequence of strings.

Once we've annotated our record with schema information, we can ask for an explanation of the schema, which is returned as data and printed:

```
user=> (require 'ch1.validate)
user=> (in-ns 'ch1.validate)
ch1.validate=> (pprint (schema.core/explain ch1.validate.Recipe))
(record
 ch1.validate.Recipe
 {:name java.lang.String,
  :description java.lang.String,
  :ingredients
  [(record
    ch1.validate.Ingredient
    {:name java.lang.String, :quantity Int, :unit Keyword})],
  :steps [java.lang.String],
  :servings Int})
```

We can also validate our data against the schema:

```
ch1.validate=> (s/check Recipe spaghetti-tacos)
nil
```

If the data is valid, s/check returns nil. If the data is invalid, s/check returns a descriptive error message detailing the schema mismatches. For example, if we passed a recipe that omitted the description and had an invalid servings value, we'd get an error message:

```
ch1.validate=> (s/check Recipe
        (map->Recipe
          {:name "Spaghetti tacos"
           :ingredients [(->Ingredient "Spaghetti" 1 :lb)
                         (->Ingredient "Spaghetti sauce" 16 :oz)
                         (->Ingredient "Taco" 12 :taco)]
           :steps ["Cook spaghetti according to box."
                   "Heat spaghetti sauce until warm."
                   "Mix spaghetti and sauce."
                   "Put spaghetti in tacos and serve."]
           :servings "lots!"}))
{:servings (not (integer? "lots!")),
 :description (not (instance? java.lang.String nil))}
```

The error message specifies the fields that didn't conform to the schema and why they failed. These checks can be a great help in detecting invalid data passed into or between parts of your program for your domain data.

Schema also has a version of defn to specify schema shapes as input parameters and return types. The types are used to create a helpful docstring:

```
ch1.validate=> (s/defn add-ingredients :- Recipe
                [recipe :- Recipe & ingredients :- [Ingredient]]
                (update-in recipe [:ingredients] into ingredients))
```

```
ch1.validate=> (doc add-ingredients)
-------------------------
ch1.validate/add-ingredients
([recipe & ingredients])
  Inputs: [recipe :- Recipe & ingredients :- [Ingredient]]
  Returns: Recipe
```

Schema can also optionally verify the runtime inputs and report schema mismatch errors by using the s/with-fn-validation function.

We've now looked at various trade-offs for representing domain entities, connecting entities together, and validating our entities. It's time to consider how we'll implement behavior for our domain types.

Domain Operations

We often need to define a function for our domain that can be applied to many different types of domain entities. This is particularly useful when domain entities of different types are collected together in a composite data structure.

Object-oriented languages typically address this need via *polymorphism*. Polymorphism is a means of abstraction, allowing a domain operation to be decoupled from the types to which it can be applied. This makes your domain implementation more general and provides a way to extend behavior without modifying existing code.

Clojure provides two features that allow the creation of generic domain operations: *multimethods* and *protocols*. Choosing the specific function to invoke for a generic operation is known as *dispatch*. Both protocols and multimethods can dispatch based on argument type, but only multimethods can dispatch based on argument value. We'll start by looking at how type-based dispatch compares in the two approaches and follow that with a look at value-based dispatch and how to layer protocols.

Multimethods vs. Protocols

Consider our recipe-manager application and the need to calculate an estimated grocery cost for each recipe. The cost of each recipe will be dependent on adding up the costs of all the ingredients. We want to invoke the same generic domain operation ("How much does it cost?") on entities of two specific types: Recipe and Ingredient.

To implement this domain operation with multimethods, we use two forms: defmulti and defmethod. The defmulti form defines the name and signature of the function as well as the *dispatch function*. Each defmethod form provides a function implementation for a particular dispatch value. Invoking the multi-method first invokes the dispatch function to produce a dispatch value, then selects the best match for that value, and finally invokes that function implementation.

We need to extend our recipe-manager domain slightly to add a Store domain entity and a function that can look up the cost of an ingredient in a particular grocery store. We can sketch these without fully implementing them:

cljapplied/src/ch1/multimethods.clj
```
(defrecord Store [,,,])

(defn cost-of [store ingredient] ,,,)
```

Now we can implement our cost multimethod for both Recipes and Ingredients:

cljapplied/src/ch1/multimethods.clj
```
(defmulti cost (fn [entity store] (class entity)))

(defmethod cost Recipe [recipe store]
  (reduce +$ zero-dollars
    (map #(cost % store) (:ingredients recipe))))

(defmethod cost Ingredient [ingredient store]
  (cost-of store ingredient))
```

First the defmulti defines the dispatch function as (class entity), which produces a dispatch value based on type. If we were using maps instead of records, we would instead extract a type attribute with (:type entity) as the dispatch function.

Once the dispatch function is invoked with an entity to produce a type, that type is matched with the available defmethod implementations, and the Recipe or Ingredient function implementation is invoked.

Now consider how we might implement this same functionality with protocols. Protocols are also defined in two steps. First, the defprotocol form declares the name and a series of function signatures (but no function implementations). Then, extend-protocol, extend-type, or extend is used to declare that a type *extends* a protocol:

cljapplied/src/ch1/protocols.clj
```
(defprotocol Cost
  (cost [entity store]))

(extend-protocol Cost
  Recipe
  (cost [recipe store]
    (reduce +$ zero-dollars
      (map #(cost % store) (:ingredients recipe))))
```

```
Ingredient
(cost [ingredient store]
  (cost-of store ingredient)))
```

Here we define the Cost protocol, which has a single function (although it could have many). We then extend two types— Recipe and Ingredient—to the Cost protocol. These are both done in a single extend-protocol for convenience, but they could be extended separately.

Let's compare these two approaches to type-based dispatch. Protocols are faster than multimethods for type dispatch because they leverage the underlying JVM runtime optimizations for this kind of dispatch (this is common in Java). Protocols also have the ability to group related functions together in a single protocol. For these reasons, protocols are usually preferred for type-based dispatch.

However, whereas protocols *only* support type-based dispatch on the first argument to the generic function, multimethods can provide value-based dispatch based on any or all of the function's arguments. Multimethods and protocols both support matching based on the Java type hierarchy, but multimethods can define and use custom value hierarchies and declare preferences between implementations when there's more than one matching value.

Thus, protocols are the preferred choice for the narrow (but common) case of type-based dispatch, and multimethods provide greater flexibility for a broad range of other cases.

Next, let's see an example of value-based dispatch with multimethods, which isn't covered by protocols.

Value-Based Dispatch

Although type-based dispatch is the most common case in many programs, value-based dispatch is needed in plenty of cases—and that's where multimethods have their time to shine.

Consider a new feature in our recipe-manager application: building a shopping list by adding together all the ingredients in one or more recipes. Ingredients are specified with a quantity and a unit. We might have some recipes that specify spaghetti in pounds and some that specify it in ounces. We need a system that can do unit conversion. Multimethods give us the ability to provide conversions that depend on the source and target types:

cljapplied/src/ch1/convert.clj

```
(defmulti convert
  "Convert quantity from unit1 to unit2, matching on [unit1 unit2]"
  (fn [unit1 unit2 quantity] [unit1 unit2]))

;; lb to oz
(defmethod convert [:lb :oz] [_ _ lb] (* lb 16))

;; oz to lb
(defmethod convert [:oz :lb] [_ _ oz] (/ oz 16))

;; fallthrough
(defmethod convert :default [u1 u2 q]
  (if (= u1 u2)
    q
    (assert false (str "Unknown unit conversion from " u1 " to " u2))))

(defn ingredient+
  "Add two ingredients into a single ingredient, combining their
  quantities with unit conversion if necessary."
  [{q1 :quantity u1 :unit :as i1} {q2 :quantity u2 :unit}]
  (assoc i1 :quantity (+ q1 (convert u2 u1 q2))))
```

The convert multimethod dispatches on the *value* of the source and target types, not on their types. Adding new conversions is then a matter of supplying a defmethod for every source/target unit pair we allow in the system.

We also provide a fallthrough case with :default—when the units are the same, we can simply return the original quantity. If the units are different and we've made it to :default, we're attempting a conversion that wasn't defined. Since this is likely a programming error, we assert that it won't happen. Missing conversions then give us a useful error while we're testing.

Here's how this looks in practice:

```
user=> (ingredient+ (->Ingredient "Spaghetti" 1/2 :lb)
                     (->Ingredient "Spaghetti" 4 :oz))
#user.Ingredient{:name "Spaghetti", :quantity 3/4, :unit :lb}
```

Here we add 1/2 pound (8 ounces) with 4 ounces and get 3/4 pound (12 ounces).

If we add new units to the system, we'll need to define conversions to and from all other units they might be combined with. In a recipe-manager application, the range of needed conversions is probably somewhat confined based on typical recipe usage.

Extending Protocols to Protocols

Both multimethods and protocols are *open systems*. Participation of a type or value in an abstraction can be specified (via defmethod or extend-protocol) separately from both the abstraction definition and the type. New participants can be dynamically added during the life of the system.

One particular case that comes up with protocols is the need to decide, at runtime, how particular concrete types should be handled in a protocol. This need commonly arises when you're creating protocols that layer over other protocols.

For example, you might need to extend the recipe manager further to calculate not only the cost of the items but also the cost of the items if bought from a particular store, including the location-specific taxes. This can be captured in a new protocol:

```
(defprotocol TaxedCost
  (taxed-cost [entity store]))
```

We already have a protocol that can make this calculation on both items and recipes of items. We'd like to layer the TaxedCost protocol over the existing Cost protocol, but this isn't allowed in Clojure:

```
(extend-protocol TaxedCost
  Cost
  (taxed-cost [entity store]
    (* (cost entity store) (+ 1 (tax-rate store)))))
;;=> exception!
```

Clojure doesn't allow protocols to extend protocols because it opens up ambiguous and confusing cases for choosing the proper implementation function. However, we can provide the same effect by detecting this case for each concrete type encountered at runtime and dynamically installing the adapted protocol for that type:

```
(extend-protocol TaxedCost
  Object                          ;; default fallthrough
  (taxed-cost [entity store]
    (if (satisfies? Cost entity)
      (do (extend-protocol TaxedCost
            (class entity)
            (taxed-cost [entity store]
              (* (cost entity store) (+ 1 (tax-rate store)))))
          (taxed-cost entity store))
      (assert false (str "Unhandled entity: " entity)))))
```

If an entity's type isn't extended to the TaxedCost protocol but *is* extended to the Cost protocol, we dynamically install an extension for the concrete type to the TaxedCost protocol as well. Once it's installed, we can then remake the same call and it'll now be rerouted to the just-installed implementation.

Note that this only happens on the *first* call with an unknown entity type. Thereafter the protocol has an extension, and it'll no longer route through Object.

Wrapping Up

You've seen how to use maps and records to model your domain entities, how to build flexible constructors for those entities, and how to connect them together.

You've also used Schema to describe and validate those entities. Clojure's approach to visible data is what makes libraries like Prismatic Schema possible. Data isn't locked inside objects but is available for annotation and processing.

Finally, you saw how to use protocols and multimethods to create generic domain operations. Generic domain operations allow us to make well-factored, extensible systems that can grow with our domain as we add both new types and new operations.

Next, you'll learn about Clojure's constructs for operating on groups of entities or other values: collections, sequences, and beyond.

## CHAPTER 2

Collect and Organize Your Data

Clojure collections are the primary means of aggregating data in Clojure and are used at all levels of a Clojure application. In this chapter we'll be focusing on how to use collections both within and around our domain model to create, update, and access our application data.

We'll begin with the basics of choosing and creating the right kind of collection for different needs. This choice is primarily driven by how we expect to use the collection after it's created.

In a number of cases we can use specialized collections or functions to update larger chunks of our collections at a time. We'll also look at some concerns about accessing the data in maps or finding items in sequential data.

We'll finish by looking at how to create a custom collection that works with the functions you've already seen. This is an advanced technique but a useful one for creating a data structure tailored to your specific application.

Choosing the Right Collection

Clojure has a small number of provided collections that are used in combination for virtually every application need. We expect that you're already familiar with the basics of the four primary Clojure collections: lists, vectors, sets, and maps.

When choosing the right collection to use, we're guided by the characteristics of the data at hand and the operations we expect to call on the collection. Clojure collection functions often specify performance constraints that must be met by the implementer.

If we need an association from a key to a value, maps are the obvious choice. In our domain model we considered the use of maps as an entity holder— as an association between entity field and value. We also saw maps used as an index from identifiers to entities in *Modeling Relationships*, on page 13. Any time we want to look up a value based on a key by using the get function, we need a map.

Clojure sets act as mathematical sets, which have the important properties of being unordered and not allowing duplicates. Sets are used primarily for situations in which it's necessary to quickly check whether a set contains a value by using contains? or get.

Most other data is sequential in nature. Clojure provides the list and vector as sequential data structures. Let's look next at how to choose between them.

Sequential Collections

Sequential data is any *ordered* series of values. For sequential data, the two primary considerations are where data will be added and removed, and whether you need *indexed* access—which concerns whether an element can be looked up by its position in the sequential collection.

Clojure lists are implemented as a linked-list data structure with each cell containing a value and a reference to the next cell. For lists, it's easy to add a new link at the beginning of the chain by creating a new cell that points to the existing list and making that the head of the list. In contrast, adding an element to the end of the list would require traversing the entire list before a new cell could be added.

One case in which a list is the best choice is when you need a *stack* (like the stack of plates at a buffet). Stacks are useful when you need to remember where you've been as you traverse a data structure (a tree or a graph). Elements are pushed on the top of the stack via cons. We can also look at the top value (with peek) and remove (with pop) the element at the top of the stack.

The Clojure vector, which can be compared in usage to an array, provides indexed access to its elements. Vectors are designed to grow at the *end* of the collection, rather than at the beginning.

Clojure operations like conj add elements at the natural insertion point—at the beginning for lists and at the end for vectors. Many new Clojure developers find it confusing that one operation behaves differently for different data structures. However, conj is designed to *efficiently* add elements at the place that's best for each data structure.

Consider choosing a collection for the recipe steps from *Model Your Domain*. If we want to retain the order as a user inserts steps, it makes the most sense to use a vector to get sequential, append-at-the-end behavior. We're likely to also find it useful to look up steps by index when we need to do things with the recipe instructions.

We now have some idea how to choose which sequential collection to use. Sequential collections are convenient because they retain their insertion order (depending on their insertion point). Clojure sets and maps are unordered, but Clojure provides sorted sets and maps for when this is important.

Sorted Collections

Sorted sets and maps allow us to specify the ordering we want to maintain across our sets or maps when data is added.

In our recipe application, we want to be able to deliver an index of authors. Authors are unique, which points to using a set. A set will automatically remove duplicates for us. We want to retain the index of authors in alphabetical order.

A sorted set uses a comparator function to determine the sort order of a pair of elements. A comparator function is applied to a pair of elements and returns a negative integer, zero, or a positive integer to indicate whether the first element should sort lower, the same, or higher than the second element in the collection.

Clojure provides a default comparator (implemented by the compare function) to give the "natural" sort order for common types of data—alphabetical for strings, ascending for numbers, and so on. The default comparator always sorts nil lower than other values. In a sorted map, the comparator applies to the keys of the map, not the values.

One common pitfall with implementing custom comparators for sorted sets and maps is that if two elements compare as the same, only one is kept and the other is removed, due to the duplicate-removal properties of the collection.

For example, a first implementation of a custom comparator for author entities might use only the last names:

```
user> (defn compare-authors-badly [s1 s2]
         (compare (:lname s1) (:lname s2)))
#'user/compare-authors-badly
user> (sorted-set-by compare authors-badly
         {:fname "Jeff" :lname "Smith"}
         {:fname "Bill" :lname "Smith"})
#{{:lname "Smith", :fname "Jeff"}}
```

Because compare-authors-badly defines equality based only on the lname field, the two author maps are seen by the set as identical and the duplicate is removed.

It's essential to ensure that two elements compare as equal only if they have the same value. One way to do this is to sort first on last name as before and then break ties by comparing each other field of the entity (here, first name):

```
user> (defn compare-authors [s1 s2]
        (let [c (compare (:lname s1) (:lname s2))]
          (if (zero? c)
            (compare (:fname s1) (:fname s2))
            c)))
#'user/compare-authors
user> (sorted-set-by compare-authors
        {:fname "Jeff" :lname "Smith"}
        {:fname "Bill" :lname "Smith"})
#{{:lname "Smith", :fname "Bill"}
  {:lname "Smith", :fname "Jeff"}}
```

This function compares entities with only two fields, but there's also a common pattern for more concisely implementing comparators that consider the fields of an entity in a custom order. This pattern relies on the mind-bending juxt function, which takes a collection of functions, creates a new function that applies all of the functions to an input, and returns a vector of the results.

Using juxt, we can apply a series of keywords as if they were getter functions and produce an ordered sequence of field values suitable for comparing.

That is, (juxt :lname :fname) produces a function that can be applied to an entity to produce a vector like ["Smith" "Jeff"]. We can then use the default compare function to compare these field vectors in natural order (from left to right).

Let's build from this. We create a local project-author function inside compare-authors that applies juxt to each author field and returns a vector for comparison:

```
user> (defn compare-author [s1 s2]
        (letfn [(project-author [author]
                  ((juxt :lname :fname) author))]
          (compare (project-author s1) (project-author s2))))
#'user/compare-authors
user> (sorted-set-by compare-author
        {:fname "Jeff" :lname "Smith"}
        {:fname "Bill" :lname "Smith"})
#{{:lname "Smith", :fname "Bill"}
  {:lname "Smith", :fname "Jeff"}}
```

This demonstrates a useful technique for creating custom entity comparators that avoid the problem of underspecification. For more detail on creating these comparators, see Andy Fingerhut's helpful comparators guide.[1]

---

1.   https://github.com/jafingerhut/thalia/blob/master/doc/other-topics/comparators.md

Now that we've examined how to choose and create the best collection for the job, let's consider the best ways to update those collections as elements are added, updated, or removed.

Updating Collections

Our applications are in constant communication with the external world, receiving new information, updating existing information, and removing information that's no longer relevant. However, this seems at odds with Clojure's immutable core collections.

In Clojure, change is always modeled as the application of a pure function to an immutable value, resulting in a new immutable value. We'll use the simple word *update* to describe this means of change so as to avoid linguistic gymnastics.

Defining collections with immutability has many advantages. First, concurrent threads can pass around values, rather than references to values. This ensures that data isn't modified unpredictably by other threads. Second, we separate our domain logic from our state- management facilities, cleanly separating concurrency concerns from our domain data and functions.

One special case that occurs with sequential data is the need to update it like a queue, also known as *first-in/first- out* processing.

First-In/First-Out Processing

Imagine a lunch counter where orders arrive from the wait staff. For fairness, we expect that orders will be filled in the order they are received —first-in/first-out (FIFO) processing.

To model the lunch counter In Clojure, we need a collection to hold the pending lunch orders. Because the lunch orders have a natural ordering in time, we know we want a sequential collection like a list or a vector to hold them. Let's try a vector:

cljapplied/src/ch2/orders.clj
```
(defn new-orders [] [])

(defn add-order [orders order]
  (conj orders order))

(defn cook-order [orders]
  (cook (first orders)) (rest orders))
```

The add-order function is adding a new order to the end of the orders, which is efficient for a vector. However, calling rest on the orders vector is inefficient:

this creates and returns a sequence (not a vector) that is all but the first element. If we wanted to retain the vector collection type, we'd need to construct a new vector and add the sequence elements back into it; all of this is expensive.

We might also implement our orders with a list. The code for cook-order would remain exactly the same, but because calling rest on a linked list is efficient, we address the performance problem we had with vectors. However, we've introduced a new problem in add-order:

cljapplied/src/ch2/orders.clj
```clojure
(defn new-orders [] '())

(defn add-order [orders order]
  (concat orders (list order)))
```

Adding an object to the end of a list requires traversing the entire list to find the final element and add a new pointer. Lists efficiently add and remove only at the beginning, and vectors efficiently add and remove only at the end—but we need a collection that adds at the end and removes at the beginning. The answer to our needs is a *queue*, as shown in the following figure.

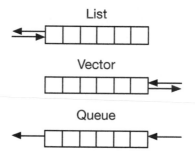

Like all of the other core collections, the queue is an immutable persistent collection, and it supports all of the same functions that you expect to work with lists and vectors. Here's how we might implement our lunch counter with a queue:

cljapplied/src/ch2/orders.clj
```clojure
(def new-orders clojure.lang.PersistentQueue/EMPTY)

(defn add-order [orders order]
  (conj orders order))

(defn cook-order [orders]
  (cook (peek orders))
  (pop orders))
```

Clojure doesn't provide a literal queue syntax or a constructor. To create a new queue, we start with the static empty instance clojure.lang.PersistentQueue/EMP-TY. In add-order we simply use conj to add new elements at the end as with a vector. In cook-order we use peek to look at the first order and pop to return all but the first order.

The queue implementation is efficient both for adding orders and for removing them in the order they were enqueued. It's the right tool for this job.

Next we'll consider how to optimize the process of adding data to collections.

Bulk Import

Clojure's persistent collections are immutable. For efficiency, adding elements via functions like conj or assoc creates a new immutable structure, but the before and after versions typically share much of their data. Because the collections are immutable, this is safe to do and much faster than copying the data. However, Clojure has a way to more efficiently fill a collection by leveraging mutability in a controlled context.

A typical case is the import of catalog items. When an application can't directly access a system of record, an export from that system can be imported into the application at start time. As the catalog changes, it's easy to imagine the need for a periodic update. For a large catalog, the process can be time-consuming.

Consider a typical import to be called when the application starts:

```
catalog-import/src/catalog_import/core.clj
(defn import-catalog [data]
  (reduce #(conj %1 %2) [] data))
```

What if we could turn on mutation and make many modifications without anyone knowing? Clojure's *transients* allow us to do this. Within a confined scope, they allow us to mutate a Clojure collection.

Call transient to get a mutable version of a vector, hash-map, or hash-set (the original stays immutable). Transient collections can't be modified by the persistent modification functions like conj and assoc. Transient collections have an equivalent set of functions that mutate the instance, all with a ! suffix: conj!, assoc!, and so on. The read interface (get, contains?, and so on) continues to work without any changes. When mutation is complete, call persistent! to get back to a persistent collection.

Here's an updated version of import-catalog that uses transient collections instead:

catalog-import/src/catalog_import/core.clj
```
(defn import-catalog-fast [data]
  (persistent!
    (reduce #(conj! %1 %2) (transient []) data)))
```

We can also check the difference in performance between the two versions by using time to check the speed when we're importing around a million catalog items, loaded into item-data as a vector of vectors:

```
catalog-import.core=> (time (import-catalog item-data)))
"Elapsed time: 129.602 msecs"
catalog-import.core=> (time (import-catalog-fast item-data)))
"Elapsed time: 110.104 msecs"
```

Transients can provide a significant boost when you're performing a bulk import. This is why Clojure's into function takes a transformation collection and determines whether it can be made transient. If so, the output collection is automatically made transient, filled using the transient functions, and turned back into a persistent collection.

Elements inside lists and vectors are typically not updated. Instead, sequential collections largely add and remove elements at the collection's insertion point. However, the internal contents of a map are frequently updated, and maps need to be transformed in some common ways.

Updating Maps

The basic tools for modifying maps are assoc and dissoc. The assoc function updates the value for a key if it's supplied with a new value. Clojure 1.7 adds an update function that can transform the value at a key based on applying a function.

For example, consider an entity (which also implements the appropriate map interfaces) describing one of the planets in our space simulation:

```
(def earth {:name       "Earth"
            :moons      1
            :volume     1.08321e12 ;; km^3
            :mass       5.97219e24 ;; kg
            :aphelion   152098232  ;; km, farthest from sun
            :perihelion 147098290  ;; km, closest to sun
           })
```

Consider adding the capability for a user to investigate the effects of adding a moon to the simulation. You can use the update function to apply the inc function, which increases the number of moons:

```
(update earth :moons inc)
```

The update function encapsulates the process of applying a function to a value inside a collection and receiving the updated collection as a result.

Sometimes you'll need to update not one but many values in a map simultaneously. Often maps representing entities will be pulled in from an external data source, such as a CSV file, JSON data, or a database. The keys may be in a different form from what you want, such as strings instead of keywords, or keywords but in the wrong namespace or case.

The Clojure core library doesn't yet contain a single function for updating every key in a map, but a number of external utility libraries provide solutions. We'll use the Medley library, which contains a small number of functions that many developers find useful.[2]

For example, consider receiving planet data from a JSON source with string keys in the following form:

```
{"name"       "Earth"
 "moons"      1
 "volume"     1.08321e12
 "mass"       5.97219e24
 "aphelion"   152098232
 "perihelion" 147098290}
```

We can change all of the keys of this entity by using the map-keys function in Medley:

cljapplied/src/ch2/update.clj
```
(:require [medley.core :refer (map-keys)])
```

cljapplied/src/ch2/update.clj
```
(defn keywordize-entity
  [entity]
  (map-keys keyword entity))

(keywordize-entity {"name"       "Earth"
                    "moon"       1
                    "volume"     1.08321e12
                    "mass"       5.97219e24
                    "aphelion"   152098232
                    "perihelion" 147098290})
;; {:name "Earth",
;;   :moons 1,
;;   :volume 1.08321E12,
;;   :mass 5.97219E24,
;;   :aphelion 152098232,
;;   :perihelion 147098290}
```

---

2. https://github.com/weavejester/medley

Perhaps even more commonly, if you use maps as indexes, you'll need to update all of the map values in a single call. The Medley library also contains a map-vals function for this purpose.

Recall that the index of recipes that we considered in *Modeling Relationships*, on page 13 was a map from recipe identifier to recipe. If we need to add calorie information to every recipe in our index, we could update the index of recipes by using map- vals as follows. We'll assume we have a compute-calories function that can produce the total number of calories for a recipe:

cljapplied/src/ch2/update.clj
```
(:require [medley.core :refer (map-vals)])
```

cljapplied/src/ch2/update.clj
```
(defn- update-calories
  [recipe]
  (assoc recipe :calories (compute-calories recipe)))

(defn include-calories
  [recipe-index]
  (map-vals update-calories recipe-index))
```

First we define an update-calories helper function that's used to compute and associate a new :calories field into a single recipe. Then, in include-calories we use map- vals to apply this function to every value in the map.

These simple functions to update all of the keys or values in a map are surprisingly useful, and most projects ultimately write or include these utilities. The implementation of these functions in Medley uses transients for improved performance—a benefit of transients that you saw in *Bulk Import*, on page 31.

Medley also includes a few other useful map transformation functions: filter-keys, filter-vals, remove-keys, and remove-vals. Collectively these allow you to either keep or remove a subset of map entries based on the result of applying a predicate function (which returns a Boolean).

Now that we've chosen our collections and filled them with data, let's consider how to get data back out of them.

Accessing Collections

The purpose of our collections is to store our data, but they're only useful if we can get the data back out of the collection. Let's first consider the collections that support indexed lookup by a key.

Indexed Access

Maps and vectors are the two indexed collections provided in Clojure. Vectors use 0-based indexes and are treated as associative collections from index to element. The records that we saw while modeling our domain also implement the map interfaces and can be treated as indexed collections.

Indexed collections support lookup by three methods. The first is by invoking the get function with the collection and a key. The second is by invoking the collection itself with a key. The third is by invoking a keyword or symbol with a collection. Here's an example of all three methods:

```
(def earth {:name "Earth" :moons 1})

(get earth :name)   ;; (1) using get
(earth :name)       ;; (2) invoking the map
(:name earth)       ;; (3) invoking the keyword key
```

All three of these methods are used in typical Clojure programs, but they have different trade-offs and are favored in different circumstances.

For entities (either maps or records), invoking the keyword as a function is the preferred method, and this style of lookup is used pervasively. The use of a keyword key as a function dovetails nicely with many of the functions in the Clojure library that take other functions as inputs.

When a map is being used as a constant lookup table of data or as a function from key to value, it's common to invoke the map as a function. One downside of this calling style is that if the map being invoked might be null, a NullPointerException will result. This is why this invocation style is most commonly seen when def has been used to create a constant global map that will never be null. Note that records are not invokable and can't be called in this way.

For any case in which it may be unclear what's happening, it's useful to invoke get directly. For example, sometimes when functions that create maps are used, it'd be confusing to invoke the return value of a function, which happens to be a lookup table.

For example, the opposite-colors function here returns a mapping of colors to contrasting colors in a particular palette.

```
(defn opposite-colors
  "Compute an opposite-color mapping for a given palette."
  [palette]
  ;; This function should compute the mapping for the palette and
  ;; return a map like this with many entries: {:magenta :green}
  )
```

Here are some calls to it:

```
((opposite-colors palette) :magenta)       ;; ok, but confusing
(get (opposite-colors palette) :magenta)   ;; less confusing
```

The first invocation example invokes the map returned by opposite-colors directly, but many Clojure readers would stumble on this usage, wondering what's happening before working it out. In general, although seeing piles of closing parentheses on the right side of an expression is common, seeing the same on the left side is relatively rare. We rarely invoke a function and then immediately invoke the return value of that function.

The second invocation example instead uses the explicit get function, which strongly signals to the reader that the value returned from opposite-colors is a map. This code also handles the case where opposite-colors returns nil, in which case get would return nil as well.

In addition to all these ways to extract a single value from a map, it's sometimes useful to extract a submap, selecting a partial set of entries. Clojure provides the select-keys function for this purpose. This function always returns a hash-map, not a map of the source type (record, sorted-map, and so on).

If we were preparing a data export from our space simulation, we could provide a simplified export that omits some of the information by selecting only a few of the most important keys:

```
(defn export-planet
  [planet]
  (select-keys planet [:name :moons]))
```

The exported planet will be a simple map: {:name "Earth" :moons 1}.

Let's turn our attention now to finding things in a sequential data structure.

Sequential Search

The maps we were working with in the last section are always the ideal choice when we want to look up a value in effectively constant time. Similarly, sets use the contains? function to quickly check whether a set contains a particular value. However, the contains? function doesn't work for finding items by value in a list or vector.

When you need an ordered sequential collection but also need to find values in that collection, you need a way to search sequentially through a collection to find a match. It's key to note that the time to undertake this search is proportional to the size of the collection —as opposed to contains?, which has the expectation of effectively constant time lookup.

One of the most common techniques seen in Clojure for sequential search is to use the some function. This function evaluates a predicate for each element of a collection and returns the first logically true value (not the original element). This is most useful with collections of simple values:

cljapplied/src/ch2/search.clj
```
(def units [:lb :oz :kg])

(some #{:oz} units)
;;=> :oz
```

The predicate being used with some is a set containing a single value. Here we're leveraging the same collection invocation style from the prior section, invoking a set as a function with each element from the units vector in turn. When a match is made, the value is returned. The result can be used as a truthy value. If no match is made, nil is returned.

The use of some for this purpose is common, but it breaks down in the specific cases of searching for nil or false, which are logically false.

A relatively efficient implementation of linear search that supports search for logically false values and will exit early can be defined as follows:

cljapplied/src/ch2/search.clj
```
(defn contains-val?
  [coll val]
  (reduce
    (fn [ret elem] (if (= val elem) (reduced true) ret))
    false coll))

(contains-val? units :oz)
;;=> true
```

We'll cover the use of reduce and reduced in detail in *Reducing to a Value*, on page 49.

Now that we've decided how to make the best use of Clojure's provided collections, we also want to consider how to solve problems unique to our own application by considering how to build our own collections.

Building Custom Collections

If none of the Clojure collections are right for your problem, you may need to roll your own. Like the standard collections, custom collections can be used seamlessly with the Clojure core library. Building a custom collection requires the use of deftype to implement the trait interfaces Clojure uses internally.

Collection Traits

If we want to build a collection that Clojure can use, we need to understand more deeply how Clojure interacts with collections. The collection and sequence libraries are based not on the particular implementations included in Clojure but on a generic set of traits that define key abstractions. Clojure collection traits are implemented internally using Java interfaces.

Predicate functions are provided in Clojure to detect the presence of the Clojure collection traits on a collection implementation. A predicate function asks a question and returns a Boolean answer, conventionally marked in Clojure with a trailing ? in the name:

Some of the predicate collection functions in Clojure are:

- counted?—Is the collection countable in constant time?
- sequential?—Are the values stored in a particular traversable order?
- associative?—Does the collection store an association between keys and values?
- reversible?—Is the collection reversible?
- sorted?—Is the collection maintained in sorted order?

These traits correspond to the following Java interfaces: Counted, Sequential, Associative, Reversible, and Sorted. Other internal interfaces define the structure of the core collection interfaces and key methods used underneath the public collection functions.

When we build a custom collection, we need to work backward, from the Clojure functions we want to implement to which Java interfaces in the implementation are required on a collection to support those functions.

The diagram on page 39 provides that mapping from Clojure function (right column) to Java method (left column). The predicate function for each interface is listed below each Java interface name.

Let's see how to take our intended usage in Clojure along with the mapping diagram to build a custom collection that satisfies our goals.

Create a Collection with deftype

Let's start with what our collection needs to do. We're going to implement a custom Pair class that holds two values we'll refer to as a and b. We'd like the Pair type to work with seq, count, nth, and get. Looking at the diagram, we see we need to implement Seqable, Counted, Indexed, and ILookup.

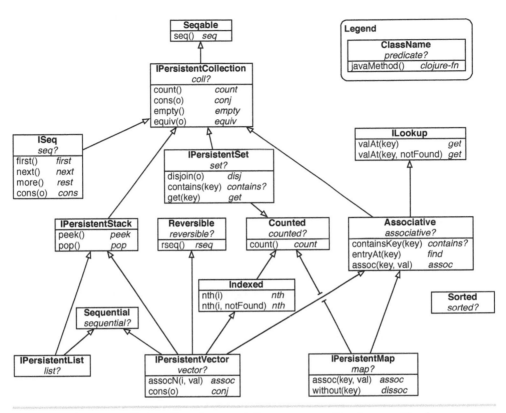

Figure 1—Clojure functions and the corresponding Java methods.

We implement a custom data structure by using the deftype macro, which looks similar to defrecord but provides more features and fewer built-in similarities to maps. For example, deftypes get a type and constructor functions as records do, but they don't automatically act like maps. With deftype, it's our responsibility to implement the proper interfaces to act like a map if we need it. Types also have support for specialized features such as mutable and unsynchronized fields, which aren't available in any other Clojure construct.

Let's see how Pair looks as a deftype:

```
cljapplied/src/ch2/pair.clj
(ns ch2.pair
  (import [clojure.lang Counted Indexed ILookup Seqable]))

(deftype Pair [a b]
  Seqable
  (seq [_] (seq [a b]))
```

```
Counted
(count [_] 2)

Indexed
(nth [_ i]
  (case i
    0 a
    1 b
    (throw (IllegalArgumentException.))))
(nth [this i _] (nth this i))

ILookup
(valAt [_ k _]
  (case k
    0 a
    1 b
    (throw (IllegalArgumentException.))))
(valAt [this k] (.valAt this k nil)))
```

Inside the deftype we list each interface being implemented and then provide the method implementation.

Now we can use the Pair type from the REPL:

```
user> (use 'ch2.pair)
nil
user> (def p (->Pair :a :b))
#'user/p
user> (seq p)
(:a :b)
user> (count p)
2
user> (nth p 1)
:b
user> (get p 0)
:a
user> p
#object[ch2.pair.Pair 0x39b4cec7 "ch2.pair.Pair@39b4cec7"]
```

Things went pretty well until we tried to look directly at p. We'll fix that now.

Custom Printing for Types

As you just saw, types have a predefined print format that contains the name of the class and an identifier. We'd like the printed form of our type to contain the instance data. The *reader* is the component inside Clojure that reads a string and returns Clojure data. Ideally we'd like our type to print in a form that can be read by the reader—this gives us full round-trip capability as a literal value.

The print apparatus is an open system with multimethods that define hooks to supply custom printers. The two hooks to consider are print- method (called when printing is done for the user) and print- dup (called when printing is done for the reader). For example, Clojure strings are printed by print-method without their surrounding quotes but in print-dup with their surrounding quotes.

For our purposes we want the Pair type to print the same in either case, so we'll implement print-dup just to call print-method:

cljapplied/src/ch2/pair/print.clj
```
(defmethod print-method Pair
  [pair ^Writer w]
  (.write w "#ch2.pair.Pair")
  (print-method (vec (seq pair)) w))

(defmethod print-dup Pair
  [pair w]
  (print-method pair w))
```

As a shortcut, in our printer we simply convert the Pair data to a vector and lean on the existing vector print-method support. Let's try it out:

```
user> (use 'ch2.pair.print)
nil
user> (->Pair 1 2)
#ch2.pair.Pair[1 2]
user> #ch2.pair.Pair[3 4]
#ch2.pair.Pair[3 4]
```

The syntax we're printing was chosen specifically because the Clojure reader uses this form to construct a Java object. The format is #class[args]. In the preceding code, if we put the constructor class syntax on the REPL, the reader will read that into a Pair object, and then the printer will print the resulting object using our print-method printer.

Wrapping Up

You now have a thorough understanding of how to use collections both within and around a domain model to collect both entities and values. Most of the data in a Clojure application is built from nothing but the collections discussed here. Occasionally you'll find it useful to build your own collection for specialized considerations or to maximize performance.

We've set the stage for how we expect to manage state in Chapter 4, *State, Identity, and Change*, on page 63. Like the concepts discussed in this chapter, state management relies heavily on the foundations of immutable values and pure transformation functions.

But first we're going to take our knowledge of collections and functions and focus on how to extend our ability to process data. So far we've been primarily working at the collection level, modifying single values or entities. Next we'll be expanding our scope to talk about sequences.

Sequences are a generalization that allows us to work with lists, vectors, and other collections as if they were sequential data structures. Most of the Clojure data-transformation capabilities are built on top of this more general abstraction, rather than being tied to specific collections. The Clojure data-transformation functions are a key part of writing powerful and reusable Clojure applications.

## CHAPTER 3

Processing Sequential Data

Once we have domain entities and collections of entities or values, we need to be able to answer questions or transform our data into new forms to satisfy our application requirements. Imperative languages often process collections by explicitly looping over a collection, but Clojure encourages thinking at the level of data in aggregate, applying transformations to a whole collection at once.

Rather than build an extensive set of functions that operate on a single data structure, Clojure builds all of its transformations on the *sequence* abstraction. Sequences are the key abstraction that connects two of the most important parts of Clojure: immutable collections and the transformation library.

By *abstraction*, we mean that only the most essential aspects of traversing a sequential source of values are included—a means of retrieving the first value, retrieving the remainder as a sequence, and checking for termination. As sequences are realized, their values are cached, allowing sequences to also be immutable regardless of their realization state. This simple abstraction is sufficient to connect almost all of the functions in the transformation library with all of the collections you've already seen.

Perhaps more important, both the participants in the sequence abstraction and the functions that operate on top of it are open systems, making this combination extensible in two dimensions (more data and more functions). Being able to connect any of our functions with any of our data enables tremendous reusability within and across Clojure programs and is a key factor in making Clojure programs concise yet expressive.

Sequences have been part of Clojure since the beginning. Clojure 1.7 introduces the concept of *transducers*. These are a further evolution of sequential processing, splitting apart the concepts of input iteration, transformation application, and output production. By separating these pieces, transducers allow further reuse of sequential transformations across an even wider variety of contexts. Throughout the chapter we'll show how sequences and transducers compare and how to make the best use of each.

Perhaps one of the most common kinds of sequence transformations is the notion of applying a function to every value in a sequence to produce a new sequence, and that's where we'll begin. Following that we'll look at some of the other common transformations: reduction to a value, filtering and removing parts of a sequence, grouping, sorting, and removing duplicates. We'll conclude by looking at using all of these transformations together to create a transformation pipeline.

Mapping Values

As data moves around your application it's common for one part of the application to need it in a different form. One subsystem imports data from a spreadsheet with 30 columns into a generic map with 30 keys. Another subsystem needs just 5 columns but in the form of an entity, and yet another system needs only a single field from a sequence of entities to perform a calculation or display it on the screen.

All of these use cases require transformation of the values in a sequential source from one form to another. In Clojure, the map function is used to apply a function to every element in a sequence and produce a new sequence of the results.

For example, consider the need to extract the orbital periods for every planet entity in our space simulation for display on the screen. Our source input is a vector of Planet domain entities, which can be treated as a sequence—logically, a list of values.

We need to transform that sequential collection of Planets to a sequential collection of orbital periods for each Planet. The orbital period is the time the planet will take for one complete orbit around the Sun. For example, on Earth the orbital period is about 365.25 days.

We can write a function to calculate the orbital period of any planet. Understanding the details of this function is not particularly important. (If you are interested the equation is shown here. T is the planet's orbital period and mu (μ) is the standard gravitional parameter.)

$$\mu = GM$$

$$T = 2\pi\sqrt{\frac{a^3}{\mu}}$$

This value depends not only on the planet in question, but also on the mass of the central star. A function that calculates the orbital period receives the planet and the star's mass as arguments and returns the orbital period:

cljapplied/src/ch3/orbital.clj
```
(defn semi-major-axis
  "The planet's average distance from the star" [p]
  (/ (+ (:aphelion p) (:perihelion p)) 2))

(defn mu [mass] (* G mass))

(defn orbital-period
  "The time it takes for a planet to make a complete
  orbit around a mass, in seconds"
  [p mass]
  (* Math/PI 2
     (Math/sqrt (/ (Math/pow (semi-major-axis p) 3)
                   (mu mass)))))
```

Now that we have a transformation function, we must use it to transform a collection of Planets to a collection of orbital periods. The Clojure map function is how we "map" every value in a sequential source to a new value, by applying a transformation function to a vector of planets.

We need a transformation function that takes one argument (the value) and returns a new value. The orbital-period function, though, is a two-argument function, so we must wrap the function we have into a transformation function of the right shape (one argument). This is often done by using an anonymous function where the constant value (the solar mass) is available in the current function scope:

cljapplied/src/ch3/orbital.clj
```
(defn orbital-periods
  "Given a collection of planets, and a star, return the
  orbital periods of every planet."
  [planets star]
  (let [solar-mass (:mass star)]
    (map (fn [planet] (orbital-period planet solar-mass)) planets)))
```

In this example, we take a collection of planets and a star, then extract the solar mass from the star. We can then call map with an anonymous function that takes the planet and invokes our orbital-period function with the planet and the solar mass. The map function walks down the collection, applying this function to every planet, and collecting the results into a sequence that's returned at the end.

Let's dive deeper into what exactly map is doing and how we've now crossed from the world of collections into the world of sequences.

Sequence Processing

The job of map is to apply a function to every value in a sequence. Let's look at a simplified version of how Clojure implements this function. We'll call our version simple-map:

```
(defn simple-map
  "Map f over the elements of coll."
  [f coll]
  (when (seq coll)
    (cons (f (first coll))
          (simple-map f (rest coll)))))
```

This implementation is written using the Clojure sequence API, which primarily consists of the seq, first, rest, and cons functions. The seq function asks whether a collection is a sequence of at least one element. If it is, it's returned; if it isn't, nil is returned. Because this result is either truthy or not, this function is often used as a condition checking for termination.[1]

When the collection being mapped has more elements, we apply the cons function. The cons function constructs a cell containing a value and a pointer to the next cell. This is the classic linked-list data structure—a series of cells containing values. The value in the first cell is defined as our transformation function f applied to the first value in the collection. The rest of the cell is defined by a recursive call back to this function, passing the same function and the rest of the input collection.

This recursive definition of the sequence is being applied to a sequential collection (a list or vector) but doesn't depend on any details of how that data structure is implemented. To implement the sequence API, a participant must only be able to check whether a next element exists, return the first element, and return a new entity for the rest of the elements. Thus, a sequence is a logical view of a collection.

In our orbital period example, we can pass any sequential collection or other implementation of the sequence API, and map will still work. The sequence abstraction has made the generic map function work across a wide range of data sources.

In general, sequence functions expect to take as input a *seqable*—something that can yield a sequence when seq is applied and also return the same. However, the result in this case will be a persistent list, which isn't as fast or

---

1. The actual map function is considerably more complicated than the version presented here, which is really for the sake of discussion. To examine the source of the actual map function, call (source map) at your REPL.

memory-efficient as the vector that was passed into the function originally. Clojure provides a special mapv function for this special case. The mapv function is identical in use to map but specifically takes and returns a vector.

This highlights a typical aspect of most sequence functions: they combine the iteration of an input source (a sequence vs. a vector), the application of the transformation (applying the f function), and doing something with the result (building a list or building a vector).

Combining these three aspects limits the ways a sequence can be used. Although the sequence input is an abstraction and can be implemented by virtually any source, it requires the creation of a cached chain of sequence nodes that may never be needed again. Similarly, this function only produces output sequences, so a different version would be needed to insert into a collection, or to push values across a communication channel instead. Transducers were introduced to take these pieces apart.

Transducers

The definition of a transducer avoids specifying where an input value comes from and how its output is used, and instead defines only the actual work the transducer is doing. In the case of map, the transducer's job is to ensure that the function is applied to every element. That essence is the same, whether the input elements come from a collection, a sequence, a socket, or a queue—and also whether the outputs are added to a collection or saved to a file.

We won't describe the implementation of transducers, because it's somewhat involved, but it's important to see how they are created and applied. To create a map transducer, omit the input collection on the call to map:

cljapplied/src/ch3/orbital.clj
```
(defn orbital-period-transformation
  "Create a map transformation for planet->orbital-period."
  [star]
  (map #(orbital-period % (:mass star))))
```

This transformation can then be used with a variety of input sources and output conditions. To produce an output sequence similar to the prior version of map, we can use this transformation with the sequence function:

cljapplied/src/ch3/orbital.clj
```
(defn orbital-periods
  [planets star]
  (sequence (orbital-period-transformation star) planets))
```

To create an output vector like the mapv version, use this:

```
cljapplied/src/ch3/orbital.clj
(defn orbital-periods
  [planets star]
  (into [] (orbital-period-transformation star) planets))
```

Or produce a list:

```
cljapplied/src/ch3/orbital.clj
(defn orbital-periods
  [planets star]
  (into () (orbital-period-transformation star) planets))
```

The versions of orbital-periods that use sequence and into differ in how they realize elements, which concerns the concept of *laziness*.

Laziness

Most Clojure sequence functions produce lazy sequences, which don't perform the transformation when the function is evaluated. Instead, the lazy sequence is evaluated only as needed by consumers of the sequence. The original sequence version of map and the transducer version with sequence both produce lazy sequences that are computed on demand.

Lazy sequences are useful in that they can avoid doing work that never needs to be computed. In this case, if no code ever consumes the lazy sequence of orbital periods, it won't ever need to be computed. Lazy sequences are also useful for representing infinite sequences of values like the Fibonacci sequence or the sequence of prime numbers. We will never (and could never) look at them all for a computation, but defining them as an infinite sequence allows us to take as many as we need for our purposes.

In contrast, into is a function that eagerly computes the entire output and returns it. Eager computations are useful because they make it easier to reason about when computation will take place. This can make it easier to manage and discard resources used by a transformation or to manage exactly when computation will occur.

In addition, the eager computation done in into is often more efficient in both memory and time. Sequences cache the values that have been computed, whereas the eager application of a transducer can often be performed on a source collection without allocating any intermediate values.

The into function is implemented in terms of the more generic reduce function, which reduces an input collection into a value.

Reducing to a Value

The reduce function reduces a collection to a value by repeatedly applying a function to an accumulated value and the next element in the collection, using an optional initial value. The into function is a special case that reduces a collection to another collection instead of a simple value.

For example, in our space simulation, consider computing the total number of moons across all planets in the solar system. We need to first extract the number of moons for each planet (a mapping transformation), then reduce those to a single value (the total) by using the + function. The reduce function is often used to combine a collection transformation with a reduction step.

We can compute the total for a collection of planets using map and reduce:

```
cljapplied/src/ch3/orbital.clj
(defn total-moons
  [planets]
  (reduce + 0 (map :moons planets)))
```

This function maps over planets, using :moons, a keyword, as a function to be applied to each Planet record. The result is a sequence of numbers representing the number of moons for each planet.

The reduce then applies the + function to each of those elements, starting with 0 as the initial accumulation value.

Because reduce produces a value, not a sequence, it's eager. The computation is thus performed when the reduce is executed.

You can also compute this transformation by using transducers and the analogous transduce function. This function differs from reduce in that it takes two functions: the transducer to be applied to each element of the input source, and the reducing function that determines what to do with the output values of the transformation. Recall that transducers intentionally break the transformation apart from both how inputs are supplied (here from a source collection) and what's done with them afterward:

```
cljapplied/src/ch3/orbital.clj
(defn total-moons
  [planets]
  (transduce (map :moons) + 0 planets))
```

This version contains many of the same elements as the prior example and is superficially similar in many ways. However, the transducer version has two potential benefits. First, the (map :moons) transducer is being used inline here but could be pulled out as a separate function and reused in any transducer context—ones that exist now or ones created in the future. That is, the transformation algorithm (simple as it may be) has been abstracted from the application of that algorithm.

Second, application of a transducer to a source will result in a single traversal of the source collection, and that traversal can sometimes take advantage of sources that know how to reduce themselves without the overhead of constructing a sequence of values.

We'll show an example of how to compose multiple transducers in the next section. Before we do that, we need to consider the special case of needing to stop reduction early, without visiting every element of the source. If given a list of Planet records, we might want to find a particular one, perhaps the one named Earth. We could implement this function as follows:

```
cljapplied/src/ch3/orbital.clj
(defn find-planet
  [planets pname]
  (reduce
    (fn [_ planet]
      (when (= pname (:name planet))
        (reduced planet)))
    planets))
```

This use of reduce doesn't pass an initial value (none is useful) and exits the reduction early when a match is found using reduced.

The anonymous function used here is called a *reducing function*. It takes two arguments: an accumulated value that's the result of the last invocation, and the new collection element being traversed. Transducers are nothing more than a means of composing reducing functions together so that a single reduction can take place instead of many.

Next let's consider how to start with an input collection and reduce the elements based on a predicate.

Filtering and Removing Values

Instead of being passed a collection of planets, we might be passed a collection of all entities in the solar system. In that case, to compute the total number of moons, we need to filter down to only the planets, then extract the moon count, and sum the moons. Let's see how this looks first with sequences:

```
cljapplied/src/ch3/orbital.clj
(defn planet?
  [entity]
  (instance? Planet entity))
```

```
(defn total-moons
  [entities]
  (reduce + 0
    (map :moons
      (filter planet?
        entities)))))
```

We've defined a planet? helper function that tests whether an entity is a Planet. In Clojure, functions that return a truthy value are are referred to as *predicates*. They're often given names that end with ?. Typically most domains you define will have a number of helper predicates.

When nesting a series of sequence transformations, you'll often find it useful to use the *thread-last* macro ->>. This macro restructures the code so that it can be read as a series of transformations in order, rather than inside-out as in the prior example.

Here's the same example rewritten with ->>, which "threads" the result of each expression into the last position of the next expression. Every sequence expression accepts the input sequence as the final argument, making this work well with most nested sequence transformations:

cljapplied/src/ch3/orbital.clj
```
(defn total-moons
  [entities]
  (->> entities
    (filter planet?)
    (map :moons)
    (reduce + 0)))
```

We can now read top-down through the function as it applies filter, then map, and finally reduce.

To achieve the same result with transducers, we now need to compose the first two transformations—filter and map—and apply them with transduce. Because each transducer wraps the prior one, like a stack, we can use comp to compose the functions in the same top-down application order as the thread-last macro:

cljapplied/src/ch3/orbital.clj
```
(def moons-transform
  (comp (filter planet?) (map :moons)))

(defn total-moons
  [entities]
  (transduce moons-transform + 0 entities))
```

After we created the composed transformation, it was easy to then invoke it from transduce. Again, several things are worth noting in comparison to the sequence version of this function. First, the composed transformation returns just the moons from just the planets in the solar system. This transformation could be reused in a different calculation in which the entities come from a different input source.

The sequence version starts with a collection of entities, then produces a smaller sequence of just planets, then finally produces a sequence of moon counts. Each intermediate sequence allocates objects and consumes memory. The transducer version uses a single compound transformation that's applied in a single pass to the source input. Here the savings are small, but in actual uses that involve a number of transformations and thousands of entities, the performance improvement is significant.

But bear in mind that in other use cases, laziness can be an important attribute. In those cases, the sequence version is preferred.

In addition to filter, some other commonly used functions for filtering the contents of a collection are remove and keep. The remove function is the opposite of filter, specifying the values to remove rather than the values that should remain. The keep function combines the capabilities of map and filter in one convenient package, applying a function to each element and keeping any non-nil results.

Take and Drop

Instead of building a subset of the collection based on a predicate, it's often useful to take or remove the beginning of a collection. In Clojure the take and drop functions can accomplish this. For example, if we receive a sequence of solar system entities from an external source, we can retrieve the nth page of results with a function like this:

cljapplied/src/ch3/fn.clj
```
(defn nth-page
      "Return up to page-size results for the nth (0-based) page
      of source."
  [source page-size page]
  (->> source
    (drop (* page page-size))
    (take page-size)))
```

This function first drops the number of pages up to the requested page, then takes the requested set of pages. The function uses sequences and doesn't realize elements beyond the requested page of results. The transducer forms will use reduced to signal early termination and also avoid realizing results beyond the requested ranges.

Sometimes, rather than just returning a page, you want both the page and the rest of the collection for further processing. The split-at helper function performs both take and drop and returns both as a tuple:

cljapplied/src/ch3/fn.clj
```
(defn page-and-rest
  [source page-size]
  (split-at page-size source))
```

This returns a vector of the first page and everything but the first page. Further processing could then invoke this again on the results after the first page.

You can also use versions of take and drop that work with predicates rather than counts: take-while and drop-while. The split-with function is the predicate equivalent to split-at.

It's often useful to combine sorting to direct the order of the elements in a collection prior to selecting a subset of elements with the take and drop functions.

Sorting and Duplicate Removal

The most basic sorting function is sort, which can sort by either the default comparator or a custom comparator if desired. For instance, this gets the first five planet names in alphabetical order:

```
(take 5 (sort (map (:name planets))))
```

In this example, we're retrieving the planet names, then sorting those names. Often, though, you want the original entities sorted by the planet's name. That is, you want to sort by a function applied to each element rather than extracting the value. This can be accomplished with sort-by:

```
(take 5 (sort-by :name planets))
```

Both sort and sort-by require materialization of their outputs so don't return lazy sequences. Neither has a transducer version.

To retrieve the smallest n planets, you need to first sort by increasing volume, then take the first n:

cljapplied/src/ch3/fn.clj
```
(defn smallest-n
  [planets n]
  (->> planets
    (sort-by :volume)
    (take n)))
```

Some nonset collections will contain duplicates. These can be removed with distinct, but this requires keeping track of the elements seen so far, a potential memory issue for large input collections. An alternative that avoids this issue with more limited capabilities is dedupe. which will remove subsequent duplicate values. The dedupe function only requires keeping the prior element in memory so is safer to use with large inputs.

Grouping Values

The helpful group-by function can group data based on a predicate, returning a map of the predicate result and a sequence of all the matches to that result. For example, we can create an index of planets by their first character:

cljapplied/src/ch3/fn.clj
```
(defn index-planets
  [planets]
  (group-by #(first (:name %)) planets))
```

This function returns a map with keys E, J, M, N, S, U, and V. Each value is a sequence of Planet entities for Earth, Jupiter, Mars and Mercury, Neptune, Saturn, Uranus, and Venus.

One common use of group-by is in combination with a predicate that returns a map of true and false keys when both are needed by the containing code.

For example, if we want to split the planets with moons from those without moons, the predicate might be this:

cljapplied/src/ch3/fn.clj
```
(defn has-moons?
  [planet]
  (pos? (:moons planet)))
```

This predicate could then be used to divide the planets into two buckets in a map:

cljapplied/src/ch3/fn.clj
```
(defn split-moons
  [planets]
  (group-by has-moons? planets))
```

Now that we've shown most of the common ways to process sequential data with Clojure, let's see what it looks like in the context of a larger example.

Putting It All Together

In many cases, processing your sequential data will follow a similar pattern:

1. *Figure out what question you're trying to ask.* This step is often the most difficult, as it sits in the problem or business domains. Once you have a clear question, Clojure provides the tools to process the data you have into an answer. That's the next three steps.
2. *Filter the data* to remove unneeded elements.
3. *Transform* the elements into the desired form.
4. *Reduce* the transformed elements to the answer.

Let's set the stage using a shopping cart example. In an online store, you have a catalog—a list of items for sale. These items are divided into departments. Customers place them in their carts, then check out. This process creates a billing record. Your client has asked for a report summarizing departmental sales: for all settled carts, what's the total sales per department?

Our domain model is as follows:

```clojure
(require '[money :refer [make-money +$ *$]])

(defrecord CatalogItem    [number dept desc price])
(defrecord Cart           [number customer line-items settled?])
(defrecord LineItem       [quantity catalog-item price])
(defrecord Customer       [cname email membership-number])
```

After many checkouts, our carts might contain a vector of #Cart records:

```clojure
[#Cart{:number 116,
       :customer #Customer{:cname "Danny Tanner",
                           :email "danny@fullhouse.example.com",
                           :membership-number 28374},
       :line-items [
         #LineItem{:quantity 3,
                   :catalog-item #CatalogItem{:number 664,
                                              :dept :clothing,
                                              :desc "polo shirt L",
                                              :amount 2515
                                              :currency :usd},
                   :price #Money{:amount 7545
                                 :currency :usd}
         #LineItem{:quantity 1,
                   :catalog-item #CatalogItem{:number 621,
                                              :dept :clothing,
                                              :desc "khaki pants",
                                              :price #Money{:amount 3500
                                                            :currency :usd},
                   :price #Money{:amount 3500
                                 :currency :usd}
       ],
       :settled? true}, ,,, ]
```

That's a pretty sizable data structure that might be easier to understand with a class diagram like the following figure.

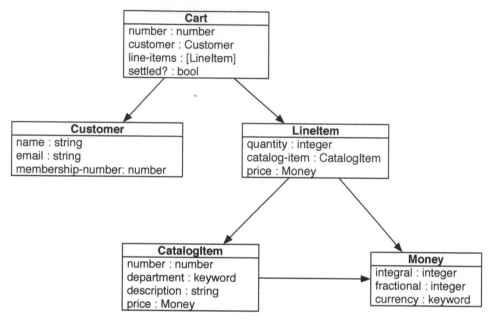

What we're looking for is much simpler—a map of departments to dollar values, something like this:

```
{:clothing #Money{:amount 2386424, :currency :usd}
 :toys     #Money{:amount 1163277, :currency :usd}
 ,,, }
```

Let's walk through the steps to get from the contents of carts to our desired output. The first thing we need to do is find the data we care about.

Selection

The selection step of sequence processing identifies and creates a subsequence containing only the elements we're interested in, which we can obtain by using filter with our cart data.

When building our report, we only want to consider carts that have been settled. Until they're settled, they're only potential revenue, not actual revenue. Begin by reducing the size of the list, using filter:

```
(defn revenue-by-department [carts]
  (->> (filter :settled? carts)
       ,,,))
```

Using the :settled? keyword as a function, we can filter out all the carts for which :settled? isn't true.

Transformation

Now that we have a sequence of settled carts, we can start separating out revenue by department. We'll discover that we don't need the cart at all—only the line items and the catalog item it contains. Let's work one step at a time for now. The next step is to create a sequence of all line items:

```
(defn revenue-by-department [carts]
  (->> (filter :settled? carts)
       (mapcat :line-items)
       ,,,))
```

The result of (mapcat :line-items ,,,) will look a lot like this:

```
[#LineItem{:quantity 3,
           :catalog-item #CatalogItem{:number   664,
                                      :dept   :clothing,
                                      :desc  "polo shirt L",
                                      :price #Money{:amount   2515
                                                    :currency :usd}},
           :price #Money{:amount   7545
                         :currency :usd}},
 #LineItem{:quantity 1,
           :catalog-item #CatalogItem{:number 621,
                                      :dept :clothing,
                                      :desc "khaki pants",
                                      :price #Money{:amount   3500
                                                    :currency :usd}},
           :price #Money{:amount   3500
                         :currency :usd}}, ,,, ]
```

The mapcat function constructs an accumulation of the contents of the line-item vectors.

Using mapcat vs. map + flatten

In place of mapcat, we could instead use map and flatten together to achieve a similar result. Whenever you're tempted to use flatten, go back one step and try to avoid creating the structure that needed to be flattened in the first place. Most commonly, this means using mapcat (to map and concatenate) rather than map.

The next step is to extract from each line item a map of the data we care about—the catalog item's :dept value and the line-item parent's :price value. We do this with map and the line-summary helper function:

```
(defn- line-summary
  "Given a LineItem with a CatalogItem, returns a map
   containing the CatalogItem's :dept as :dept and LineItem's :price
   as :total"
  [line-item]
  {:dept  (get-in line-item [:catalog-item :dept])
   :total (:price line-item)}})

(defn revenue-by-department [carts]
  (->> (filter :settled? carts)
       (mapcat :line-items)
       (map line-summary)
       ,,,))
```

We're almost there! Now we have a sequence of maps that contain *only* the data we need to report on:

```
[{:dept :clothing :total #Money{ ,,, }
 {:dept :clothing :total #Money{ ,,, }
 {:dept :toys     :total #Money{ ,,, }
 {:dept :kitchen  :total #Money{ ,,, }
 {:dept :toys     :total #Money{ ,,, }]
```

From here, we can use group-by to construct a map with the department as the key and a sequence of summaries as the values:

```
(defn revenue-by-department [carts]
  (->> (filter :settled? carts)
       (mapcat :line-items)
       (map line-summary)
       (group-by :dept)
       ,,,))
```

At this point, our data looks like this:

```
{:clothing [{:dept :clothing :total #Money{},
            {:dept :clothing :total #Money{}, ,,,]
 :toys     [{:dept :toys     :total #Money{},
            {:dept :toys     :total #Money{}, ,,,]
 :kitchen  [{:dept :kitchen  :total #Money{}, ,,,]}
```

We could take on an extra step to replace the summaries with a vector of the #Money{} values in the :total, but it's unnecessary. Instead, let's move on to our final step: summarizing those values.

Reduction

As with our line-summary function, we probably want to define a function to handle totaling each department that our reducing process can use:

```
(require '[money :refer [make-money +$ *$])

(defn- dept-total
  [m k v]
  (assoc m k (reduce +$ (map :total v))))

(defn revenue-by-department [carts]
  (->> (filter :settled? carts)
       (mapcat :line-items)
       (map line-summary)
       (group-by :dept)
       (reduce-kv dept-total)))
```

Within our piecewise dept-total function, we can see a microcosm of our usual sequence-processing pipeline. In this case, map selects the :total from each element of the sequence, then reduce +$ sums it up.

You may find this alternative implementation of dept-total using the thread-last macro easier to read:

```
(defn- dept-total*
  [m k v]
  (assoc m k (->> (map :total v)
                  (reduce +$))))
```

That's it. We've reduced our initial vector of carts to a map of revenue by department. Our final data is in this shape, as promised:

```
{:clothing #Money{},
 :toys     #Money{},
 :kitchen  #Money{}, ,,, }
```

The data pipeline we've gone through in this section is fairly typical: select, transform, reduce. It's perhaps best for you to think of this as a unit of sequence processing. As you saw with the dept-total function, one unit of sequence processing can enclose an entire other unit. As your practice develops, creating smooth pipelines will become more reflexive.

Another important thing to note, made obvious by our use of the thread-last macro (->>) in the revenue-by-department function: a sequence goes into and out of each step of the process. In fact, in the first three steps (filter, mapcat, and map), each element of the starting sequence could make it through all three steps successfully before the next element begins, and the results would be the same. Those steps operate on a single element of the sequence at a time, without consideration for anything that's gone before or anything following. This is a good clue that using a transducer is also an option for this part of the pipeline.

Wrapping Up

Clojure collections provide the immutable base for Clojure data, and sequences provide a key abstraction over both collections and any other sequentially traversable data source. We've shown the most common means of processing sequential data using both sequence functions and transducers.

Transducers gain better performance and more reusabilility by splitting the sequence-processing model into source iteration, transformation, and output processing such that they can be altered independently. You saw the use of sequence, into, and transduce as three common means of applying transducers to an input source. In future chapters we'll also show how to apply these same transducer functions in core.async channels.

Now that we've modeled our domain, grouped those domain entities into collections, and processed them, we need to consider how to start collaborating state across threads and time.

Part II

Applications

The Clojure model of state builds on the foundations of immutable data and update functions. This state model forms the basis for Clojure reference types. Given a way to safely share state, concurrent and parallel programming become safe, efficient, and straightforward.

Clojure components package data, transformations, state, and concurrency into larger units of code. These units can then be assembled into applications.

## CHAPTER 4

State, Identity, and Change

You have entities, collections of data, domain functions, and some useful patterns for processing sequential data under your belt. It's time to start thinking about the continuity of domain data during the execution of an application.

This means that you should be thinking about the identity and state of your domain entities, and how identities within your domain are related. Creating coherent state management in your domains will prepare your application for the concurrent operations we'll explore in Chapter 5, *Use Your Cores*, on page 85.

In this chapter, you'll learn to apply Clojure's tools for managing changes in state for entities in your domain. More fundamentally, we'll look at identity and state as separate things. Clojure is designed to take advantage of the multicore state of the computing world. You'll find some practical advice for choosing strategies for state management and learn to recognize some of the pitfalls that mutability can introduce in light of a multithreaded program.

Let's begin with an overview of what state and identity mean in the context of a Clojure application.

Modeling a Change

Recall that Clojure's focus is on immutable values. With immutable data, an "update" produces a new instance of an entity (or collection of entities), rather than updating the entity or entities in place. In most cases, this will serve your purposes admirably. Occasionally, you'll need to model the changes in the application's world, to track changes in data. Specifically, you want to hold onto a reference to a set of data that changes.

In a multithreaded scenario, updating data in place introduces a lot of complex questions. Who can change the data? How do other threads get notified of the change? Which process wins when multiple simultaneous updates are happening? Clojure provides elegant answers to all of these questions via its state-management tools. To use these tools effectively, you must first understand Clojure's approach to identity and state.

Seeing in Snapshots

To help you arrive at that understanding, let's talk for a minute about time. Although the human experience seems continuous, your senses collect information into discrete quanta. Sounds, sights, and smells enter your brain independently, then are correlated into moments in time. As you play through those moments in succession, you experience the illusion of a continuous perception.

If you were to view your visual quanta, we would see a series of snapshots similar to the "Sallie Gardner at a Gallop" series by Eadweard Muybridge, shown in the following figure.

Muybridge snapped these photographs in 1878 to determine if all four of a horse's hooves ever leave the ground simultaneously. The apparent movement that they capture is illusory, but our minds apply continuity. We play through the pictures in the sequence and see Sallie Gardner's historic run.

Imagine representing this series as an entity recording the number of hooves that reach the ground. The initial update would have one hoof down, the second zero, and so on until we reached the last picture.

If you can see only a single set of values, you lose the very thing that makes this series interesting. Not only can you no longer clearly picture the movement of the horse, but the original question would remain unsettled in all frames save the second and third. You lose the dimension of time.

Similarly, if you approach changing data as an object-oriented programmer, you'll tend to model the data in the world as objects. When the world changes, the objects representing that world are updated in place, yielding a model of the world that reflects the now. The problem with this approach is that it leaves the viewer with only that last frame.

Sometimes this behavior is exactly what you want: a single thread concerning itself with the result of a series of steps—systems for which the *now* view is the only view. When by habit you only concern yourself with the now, however, it's easy to conflate two concepts: *identity* and *state*. Let's spend a little time disentangling the two.

Understanding Identity and State

Consider your favorite coffee shop. Depending on the time of day, it might be open or closed. As new roasts come through the door, the available brews change. Different shifts have different baristas manning the espresso machine and a different set of customers at the bar. The coffee shop might even change its location or name at some point. Even with all this change, the identity of the coffee shop remains the same. The shop's *identity* wraps around and enfolds the different coffees, clientele, staff, and whether the door is locked when you need your morning joe.

State, on the other hand, represents an identity's value for a instant in time. To continue our coffee shop analogy, at 7 a.m. on Tuesday the shop is open, Lindsay is managing the register, Jimmy is dialing in the grinder, the customers are checking their laptops before heading to the office, and the light roast is something Ethiopian.

By considering the morning shift you can see that state and identity are two separate things. A state is a value or set of values belonging to an identity. Identity is a series of states, separated by time. At any moment, we might ask questions like, which dark roast coffee is being served? or, are any seats available? To get an accurate response when you ask, updates must happen in an orderly way, or else we might find ourselves unexpectedly sitting on someone's lap.

To make this work we not only need mutability; we also need that update to occur discretely and instantaneously from the point of view of an observer. That is, for a given identity, we need the ability to make a change to that identity's data that becomes visible to all observers at the same time.

Updates in Succession

In Clojure, we can create references to identities with values we want to update. Generally, a reference is a mutable container for a succession of immutable values. Clojure calls its approach to managing values that change over time the *unified update model*. The unified update model generally follows this form:

```
(update-fn container data-fn & args)
```

The data-fn in this case is applied to the currently stored value in the reference, creating a new value. This new value succeeds and replaces the current value being held by the reference. All reference types (*var*, *atom*, *agent*, and *ref*) use this model to implement successive data. However, each type has its own semantics.

Which reference type you use to hold each identity depends on what properties you want your updates to have. For the moment, let's focus on atomic vs. transactional succession, both of which implement the unified update model. In both of these cases, the identity's value can always be read.

Atomic Succession

Atomic succession updates a single identity. Given an update function and an identity, the function is applied to the current value of the identity. If all goes well, the result replaces the current value. Possible complications arise when another thread updates the identity's value while the update function executes. Clojure handles this by retrying the function on the new value until it either succeeds or reaches the retry limit.

You'll use atomic succession when you have a stand-alone value (or composite value) that can change independently of the rest of your system. Although atomic updates can inform other system values and functions when they complete (via watch functions), the values they hold don't require coordination with other stateful references.

Collections make good candidates for atomic succession: inventory, employee registry, a list of input or output channels, and so on. You'll see an example that uses inventory in the next section.

In Clojure, atomic succession has both synchronous and asynchronous representations in the atom and agent, respectively. We'll get down to brass tacks with the atom in a moment; agents are covered on page 87.

Transactional Succession

If you require that two identities update *together*, then you'll want to use transactional succession. As the name implies, this involves a *transaction* to ensure that either all or none of the coordinated updates happen.

Generally, a transaction consists of a set of coordinated changes to a set of identities. A single identity can be involved in multiple transactions at a time. As with atomic succession, Clojure resolves conflicts via a number of retries. Unlike with atomic succession, because many identities are involved the entire transaction is retried. Rather than a single update to one independent identity, a transaction can contain many updates to several coordinated identities.

Inside the Transaction

A transaction is a tiny bubble of your application's reality. Within the bubble, identities behave as though the transaction has been successful so far: values read from identities are current within the transaction's timeline, and updates can be applied to adjust these values.

Before the transaction completes and commits changes back to the application, Clojure checks to see if any of the identities involved in the transaction have been updated outside the bubble. If they have, it reads in the latest set of values for the identities and retries the transaction. Otherwise, the transaction commits, and the bubble pops.

For the curious who haven't already read *Programming Clojure (2nd edition) [HB12]*, Clojure accomplishes this using software transactional memory (STM)[1] implementing the multiversion concurrency control (MVCC)[2] model.

We've spoken about atomic and transactional succession in a general way so far. Now let's get to the particulars—tools and code you can actually use.

---

1. http://en.wikipedia.org/wiki/Software_transactional_memory
2. http://en.wikipedia.org/wiki/Multiversion_concurrency_control

Tools for Managing Change

Clojure has four reference types (var, atom, agent, and ref) that we can use to store application state. In every case, the mechanism provides a mutable container storing an immutable value. We can create the container with an initial value and reset that value. We can also advance the state using the unified update model. In this fashion, we can change the application state in a managed way.

Clojure's reference types implement IRef. The following table lists those types along with their create, update, and reset functions:

IRef	create-fn	update-fn(s)	set-fn
Atom	atom	swap!	reset!
Ref	ref	alter, commute	ref-set
Var	def	alter-var-root	var-set
Agent	agent	send, send-off	restart-agent

The pattern for all of these reference types is similar:

```
;; to create:
(create-fn container)

;; to update:
(update-fn container data-fn & args)

;; to assign a value:
(set-fn container new-val)
```

For agents, you can include error-handling options when creating the agent.

A var stores mutable data in local memory and isn't managed. Atoms limit changes to their stored value via synchronous transformation (using swap!) but don't coordinate these changes. Refs provide controlled transformation of their stored values through STM. An agent stores individual application state but updates asynchronously. (We'll cover agents in *Use Your Cores*.) In this section, we'll provide an overview of atoms, refs, and vars, with examples to demonstrate their use.

Let's turn our attention first to managing changes using atoms and refs.

Managed Updates with Atom

When our data begins to be observed by multiple threads, it becomes necessary to protect those threads from the chaos of uncoordinated and partial updates. Failure to do so can leave our system in an invalid state.

Let's Go Shopping

Let's walk through a thought exercise about how best to coordinate activities. Each time you're deciding on a concurrent implementation, you'll go through a similar exercise to help you decide what information to manage and what information you can leave unmanaged.

To get some practice, let's go grocery shopping. First we'll consider grocery shopping in a single-threaded way, then build upon those needs for a more complex, multithreaded example. As we proceed, we'll add various transactional memory mechanisms until we have something useful.

The Solo Operator

We know how grocery shopping works. You make a list, then go to the store and buy the things on the list. For a single person, this is pretty straightforward. The person who makes the list is the one who heads to the store:

```
shopping/src/shopping/single.clj
(defn go-shopping-naive
  "Returns a list of items purchased"
  [shopping-list]
  (loop [[item & items] shopping-list
         cart []]
    (if item
      (recur items (conj cart item))
      cart)))
```

This scenario requires no state management. One thread (person) follows a list and returns a cart full of delicious junk food. At least that's how it works when you're in college.

In this example, everything rests on an infinite shelf. We're simply moving things from one list to another. In a more complete representation we would represent the store's inventory, and our college student might discover that his dorm-mates got to all the pizza first. Let's write an API so that we can interact with that inventory in a managed way.

Building Our Store API

We represent our store's inventory with a map of items to quantities. We can expect that multiple threads may be operating on this inventory, so we need to ensure that any observer sees consistent data. This can be implemented with an atom.

An atom is a *synchronized* construct. That is, by using an atom, we ensure that every change we inflict on the atom happens completely before the next one is applied. An atom is also *independent*, or uncoordinated. We'll talk a little more about coordination in the next section. Finally, an atom updates *immediately*. In addition to the store itself, let's define grab and stock functions to give shape to our budding API:

shopping/src/shopping/store.clj

```
Line 1  (ns shopping.store)

        (def inventory (atom {}))

     5  (defn no-negative-values?
          "check values of a map for a negative value"
          [m]
          (not-any? neg? (vals m)))

    10  (defn in-stock?
          "check if an item is in stock"
          [item]
          (let [cnt (item @inventory)]
          (and (pos? cnt))))
    15
        (defn init
          "set up store with inventory"
          [items]
          (set-validator! inventory no-negative-values?)
    20    (swap! inventory items))

        (defn grab
          "grab an item from the shelves"
          [item]
    25    (if (in-stock? item)
            (swap! inventory update-in [item] dec)))

        (defn stock
          "stock an item on the shelves"
    30    [item]
          (swap! inventory update-in [item] inc))
```

Using the atom function, we declare that inventory is an atom, and that changing its value is restricted to functions that allow its changes to be managed. These functions are swap!, reset!, and at a somewhat lower level, compare-and-set!.

Since the inventory's value is stored inside an atom, to view the value, we must dereference it with (deref inventory) or @inventory. When we change the value of the atom, under the covers Clojure does the following:

1. Dereferences (and saves) the current value
2. Invokes the function passed to swap!
3. Validates the new value or throws an exception

4. Compares and sets:

    - If the current value of the reference hasn't been changed (for example, by another thread), replaces with the result of the function invocation and returns the new value
    - If the current value has been changed during the method invocation, doesn't replace the value, and starts over

Guarding Against Invalid State

The swap! method repeats until it completes its mission; we're guaranteed to invoke our function against a complete snapshot of the data. We're not, however, guaranteed to invoke our function against the value the atom held at the time the swap! was called. Without the validator we define on line 16, it would be entirely possible to end up with negative :bacon, and nobody wants that. Let's look at an example of this kind of unfortunate timing:

```
(:bacon @inventory)                          ; => 1
(if (in-stock? item)                         ; thread 1
(if (in-stock? item)                         ; thread 2
    (swap! inventory update-in [item] dec))) ; thread 2
    (swap! inventory update-in [item] dec))) ; thread 1
(:bacon @inventory)                          ; => -1
```

As you can see, the timing of the guard matters. To avoid negative inventory, we need to add some insurance on line 19 by passing in a *validator* function. Using a validator, we can ensure that the minimum value an inventory item can have is 0.

Before the value of the atom is changed, the proposed new value is passed to the validator function. If the validator function returns false, attempts to change the atom will throw an IllegalStateException. The validator function can also throw an exception of its own, which takes the place of the IllegalStateException. Where this is possible (for example, when calling the grab function from line 22 of store.clj), that possibility must be handled. In general, a validator must be a side effect–free function (or nil) taking a single argument. Recall that it can be called many times.

(We could just as easily have declared the validator function when we defined our inventory:

```
(def inventory (atom {} :validator no-negative-values?))
```

This is especially useful when you're passing in an initial state. The validator validates the initial state when the atom is created.)

Now that we can use our emergent store API and replace the loop with a reduce, we're left with a much cleaner approach. This code replaces the go-shopping-naive function:

```
shopping/src/shopping/single.clj
(defn shop-for-item [cart item]
  "Shop for an item, return updated cart"
  (if (store/grab item)
    (conj cart item)
    cart))

(defn go-shopping
  "Returns a list of items purchased"
  [shopping-list]
  (reduce shop-for-item [] shopping-list))
```

Notice that even in this simple example, the API starts to take shape after a few well-considered steps. This should be happening everywhere, all the time. Think, then do, and tiny wonders emerge.

Watching Inventory

To keep our college student in ramen noodles week after week, the store must periodically restock. The items to restock could be kept in a master list or a config file and refreshed periodically, but that can involve worrying about scheduling. Instead, why not consider adding a *watch function*?

Watches exist—as one might expect—to keep an eye on things. They're comparable to an implementation of the Observer design pattern in an object-oriented language and serve much the same purpose. However a watch has less overhead: Clojure handles registration and notification of watches, so that the watcher function remains a simple function—specifically, a function of four arguments: a key, a reference to watch, the old value, and the new value.

Watches can apply to all reference types. A single reference can have multiple watchers, each holding a different key, all of which are updated when the value referred to changes.

An example, you say? Let's use a watch function to notify the store when an item leaves the inventory:

```
shopping/src/shopping/store.clj
Line 1  (declare sold-items)

     -  (defn restock-order
     -    "a watch to restock an item"
     5    [k r ov nv]
```

```
       (doseq [item (for [kw (keys ov)
                          :when (not= (kw ov) (kw nv))] kw)]
         (swap! sold-items update-in [item] (fnil inc 0))
         (println "need to restock" item)))

10
     (defn init-with-restock
       "set up store with inventory"
       [m]
       (def inventory (atom m))
15     (def sold-items (atom {}))
       (set-validator! inventory no-negative-values?)
       (add-watch inventory :restock  restock-order))
```

We've changed our initializer and added a watch function on line 17. A watch function takes the following form:

```
(defn watch-fn [watch-key reference old-value new-value] ,,,)
```

This method is called whenever the atom's value updates successfully. It compares the old inventory value to the new inventory value and extracts the items that have changed into a new atom, sold-items. Since we know that grab pulls out only one item at a time, we can be satisfied with a simple increment.

Watch functions take four parameters: a key for the function, the reference being watched, the old value, and the new value. The last three are straightforward, but the key (for example, :restock) can be opaque. Under the covers, the key identifies the watch function in the hash-map of watch functions attached to the reference (retrievable with the .getWatches function). It can be used by remove-watch to remove a watch function and by add-watch to replace an existing watch function. You can generally treat the key as a label and not worry too much about it.

Since we can now detect when an item is removed from the shelves, let's restock them.

Restocking the Shelves

Once we've started keeping track of the items we've sold, we might want to restock our shelves periodically. Here we'll implement a fairly unsophisticated restocking scheme. We reset both our inventory and our sold items:

shopping/src/shopping/store.clj
```
Line 1  (defn restock-all
   2      "restock all items sold"
   3      []
   4      (swap! inventory #(merge-with + % @sold-items))
   5      (reset! sold-items {}))
   6      ; be careful, here be dragons.
```

But wait! In making this overly simple, we've missed a few important things. When we use our store API, they become readily apparent:

```
user=> (use ['shopping.store :as 'store])
nil
user=> (store/init-with-restock {:apples 1 :bacon 3 :milk 2})
#<Atom@eb74118: {:bacon 3, :apples 1, :milk 2}>
user=> (store/grab :bacon)
need to restock :bacon
user=> (store/grab :bacon)
need to restock :bacon
{:bacon 1, :apples 1, :milk 2}
user=> (store/grab :milk)
need to restock :milk
{:bacon 1, :apples 1, :milk 1}
user=> @store/sold-items
{:milk 1, :bacon 2}
user=> @store/inventory
{:bacon 1, :apples 1, :milk 1}
user=> (store/restock-all)
need to restock :bacon
need to restock :milk
```

The last two printed lines in the preceding session demonstrate one of our oversights. When we used swap! within restock-all to update our inventory, the watch function was called, generating two new entries into our list of items sold. Why two and not three? Because our watch function wasn't designed to look for changes in quantity, only to record the name of the item grabbed. The same thing would've happened had we called stock.

Our other oversight remains a little more obscure. Remember that we're trying to understand our world in a concurrent way. In our restock-all function, we've left a gap for chaos to enter, just before line 5. If another thread were to grab an item from the inventory at that time, that item's entry in our sold-items atom would be wiped out, and the next time we restocked, we'd be short an item.

In this case, our choice of atom for an inventory container has broken down. In this implementation, inventory was intended to be tracked independently and synchronously. When we add a second item-tracking mechanism into our state, we suddenly need things to coordinate. Coordinating even a small number of things can get tricky. We can address this trickiness with refs.

Transactional Change with Ref

For more-complex domains, where concurrent updates to several values must be coordinated, atoms no longer work. We need the power of transactions, and that needs a series of refs. Let's show this with a complex shopping trip.

Shopping with a Pack

If you have children, you might bring them along to help you fill your cart. This will require some coordination, so we need to decide what approach will work best.

In a simple scenario, we divide our shopping list among the children, then send them out to collect the items on their lists. They return when they've completed their shopping, and we combine the items at the end.

Problem solved, right? We took care of our coordination problem up front through a division of labor, after which no cooperation was required. State management: avoided.

Of course, this assumes that all of our children have the same attention span and will do their best to find the items on their lists, not get distracted, and not bring anything else back. If all of this is true, then we can expect things to go swimmingly. A more realistic implementation of a child's approach to shopping might look like this:

```
shopping/src/shopping/family_async.clj
(defn dawdle
  "screw around, get lost, maybe buy candy"
  []
  (let [t (rand-int 5000)]
    (Thread/sleep t)
    (maybe? buy-candy)
    ))
```

We've added a little chaos, which we'll need to mitigate. We send each child out to find one item, and they dawdle for some length of time. When they return, they put their assigned item—and maybe some candy—in the cart and receive their next assignment. Our more focused gophers will do more work, but the items get crossed off the list eventually.

Building Transactions from Rules

The key to success here is to have clear rules about the items being shopped for. Given those rules, we want to model and update the state in such a way that the rules can be followed.

The rules are straightforward:

- An item in the shopping list gets crossed off when it's assigned to a child.
- An item remains assigned to a child until it's placed in the cart.
- Candy isn't allowed in the shopping list or in the cart.

To preserve our rules, assigning an item to a child and removing it from the shopping list must occur simultaneously from the point of view of our local world. Likewise, recovering the item and placing it in the cart must effectively be simultaneous. We need to coordinate these actions; for that we'll need a ref or three.

A ref stores its value in the ref world and can help us ensure that changes to its value are performed transactionally in a coordinated, synchronous fashion. In the following example, we create three refs. The shopping-list is a set holding the items we intend to shop for. We track the items in flight with the assignments map, using the child's name as the map key. Finally, the shopping-cart is a set of items we've recovered from a child:

```
shopping/src/shopping/family_async.clj
(def shopping-list (ref #{}))
(def assignments (ref {}))
(def shopping-cart (ref #{}))

(defn init []
  (store/init {:eggs 2 :bacon 3 :apples 3
               :candy 5 :soda 2 :milk 1
               :bread 3 :carrots 1 :potatoes 1
               :cheese 3})
  (dosync
    (ref-set shopping-list #{:milk :butter :bacon :eggs
                             :carrots :potatoes :cheese :apples})
    (ref-set assignments {})
    (ref-set shopping-cart #{})))
```

Changing the value of a ref must be done inside a transaction, using dosync. A transaction can be composed of many updates.

These updates come in three flavors. To update the value of a ref directly, we use ref-set. When updating using a function, we use either alter or commute. Most frequently, you'll see ref-set in the context of reinitialization.

Using alter requires that the value of the ref when the function is applied be the same as the value of the ref either when the transaction began, or when the last alter function was applied within the current transaction. If the ref was updated by a concurrently running transaction during the execution of this transaction, it triggers a retry. If your transaction needs to run without outside interference, alter is the function you should use.

If your transaction doesn't require a check on internal consistency, commute can be used. The commute function doesn't trigger a retry when the value of the ref has been changed in the course of the transaction's execution. The function passed to commute is executed on whatever value the ref has at the time.

In a high-concurrency application, replacing alter calls with commute where possible can improve performance by avoiding retries. This should only be done when the function passed to commute is commutative—that is, when the result of applying the update function yields the same result regardless of the order in which it's executed. Think of addition: (4 + 6 + 2) is the same as (2 + 4 + 6).

The ensure function can be used to ensure that a ref's value hasn't changed outside of the current transaction without updating it. If ensure discovers that the value has changed, it triggers a retry. This is useful in situations where refs have interdependent values. For example, when completing a purchase, we might ensure on a price list to ensure that prices haven't changed during the transaction, even though we're not updating the price. A changing price mid-transaction should trigger a retry.

To briefly review the syntax of updating a ref: we alter (or commute) a ref by sending a function and args responsible for making the update.

The next block of code defines the functions we'll need to perform transactional activities. Once again, we can see an API start to precipitate out of our code. The assign-item-to-child function removes an item from the shopping list and assigns it to a child. The collect-assignment function adds the shopped-for item to the shopping cart and discards the child's assignment. Our dawdle function from earlier uses buy-candy. Here are our transactions:

```
shopping/src/shopping/family_async.clj
(defn assignment
  [child]
  (get @assignments child))

(defn buy-candy []
  (dosync
   (commute shopping-cart conj (store/grab :candy))))

(defn collect-assignment
  [child]
  (let [item (assignment child)]
    (dosync
     (alter shopping-cart conj item)
     (alter assignments dissoc child)
     (ensure shopping-list) ;; not needed
                            ;; included as an example
     )
    item))
```

```
(defn assign-item-to-child [child]
  (let [item (first @shopping-list)]
    (dosync
      (alter assignments assoc child item)
      (alter shopping-list disj item))
    item))
```

The preceding methods both operate on two different elements of state that need to update completely before local control returns. These methods use alter to update the collections that will be changing, indicating that the operations are to be executed in that order. The methods also use ensure to protect the refs that weren't updated.

While the transaction (dosync) is running, writes to the refs identified in our dosync block are prevented. All these changes get proposed, then committed in the ref world, our alternative timeline. If everything finishes successfully, all updates will be readable in the local world after the write point. Otherwise, no changes are committed and the transaction is retried until it reaches the retry limit (as of this writing: 10,000). This ensures that our rules are maintained for all running threads.

Making the Trip

Now that we have our transactional methods defined, we can actually go shopping:

shopping/src/shopping/family_async.clj
```
(defn send-child-for-item
  "eventually shop for an item"
  [child item q]
  (println child "is searching for" item)
  (dawdle)
  (collect-assignment child)
  (>!! q child))

(defn report []
  (println "store inventory" @store/inventory)
  (println "shopping-list" @shopping-list)
  (println "assignments"   @assignments)
  (println "shopping-cart" @shopping-cart))

(defn go-shopping []
  (init)
  (report)
  (let [kids (chan 10)]
    (doseq [k my-kids]
      (>!! kids k))
    (go-loop [kid (<! kids)]
```

```
(if (seq @shopping-list)
  (do
    (go
      (send-child-for-item kid (assign-item-to-child kid) kids))
    (recur (<! kids)))
  (do
    (println "done shopping.")
    (report))))))
```

If the go-loop and strange alien alphabet pieces (<!, >!!) look unfamiliar, don't worry—they're a part of core.async, which we'll be covering in more detail when we talk about concurrency in Chapter 5, *Use Your Cores*, on page 85. For now, know that we take a child from the queue (called a channel) when we begin the loop, and return that child to the queue once we've collected that child's assigned item.

Apart from that, the shopping itself proceeds fairly intuitively. By keeping our transactions as simple as possible and in as few places as possible, we mitigate a lot of our risk of chaos.

Oh, but we didn't address the candy. The rules say no candy, so let's add that validator to our shopping cart:

shopping/src/shopping/family_async.clj
```
(def shopping-cart (ref #{}
  :validator #(not (contains? % :candy))))
```

Alternatively, if we don't want the cart to explode when candy inevitably finds its way in, we could just add a watch function that notifies a parent when that happens, delaying any decisions concerning punishment:

shopping/src/shopping/family_async.clj
```
(defn notify-parent
  [k r _ nv]
  (if (contains? nv :candy)
    (println "there's candy in the cart!")))
```

Once the watch function is created, we add it to our shopping-cart in init:

shopping/src/shopping/family_async.clj
```
(add-watch shopping-cart :candy notify-parent)
```

Last but not least, let's consider the var container.

Tracking Local State with Var

Finally, not all state requires management. Data that won't be changing (such as *system state*) doesn't require change control. Likewise, data that won't be observed by other threads doesn't need management. In these cases, we use a var to store our data. We set a var using def:

```
user=> (def my-kids #{:alice :bobby :cindi})
```

This var has global scope with a symbol (my-kids) in the current namespace. If that var already exists, it's set to the new value. We can read and redefine this var however we please. We update vars using alter-var-root. Pay attention to the #' fiddly bit in front of my-kids: we pass the var itself—not its value—to alter-var-root:

```
user=> (defn born! [new-kid] (alter-var-root #'my-kids conj new-kid))
#'user/born!
user=> (born! :donnie)
#{:donnie :alice :bobby :cindi}
```

If we want to allow a var to be redefined in a local binding or thread without compromising its global definition, we can add metadata to have this effect when defining it:

```
user=> (def ^:dynamic my-kids #{:alice :bobby :cindi})
#'user/my-kids
user=> (print my-kids)
#{:alice :bobby :cindi}
user=> (binding [my-kids #{:luke :leia}]
#_=>      (print my-kids))
#{:leia :luke}
user=> (print my-kids)
#{:alice :bobby :cindi}
```

Vars are stateful, but they're stored in local memory and as such aren't *managed*. When we add dynamic scope to a var we localize its binding but encounter other problems. Stuart Sierra has written an article on this problem, called "On the Perils of Dynamic Scope."[3] In short, don't do this unless you really mean it and know what you're doing.

We've walked through most of the main constructs Clojure provides for managing changes to your application's state with ref and atom, and their associated update functions. We also briefly reviewed var for storing global state. Now that we have tools for managing change, we should take a moment to talk about how we might go about living with change.

In the next section, you'll learn how to make good implementation decisions concerning managed change, and two approaches to growing your APIs while limiting the influence of mutability.

---

3.   http://stuartsierra.com/2013/03/29/perils-of-dynamic-scope

Living with Change

We've examined in detail several tools that Clojure provides for making updates to our application's state. These tools guard against misadventure by ensuring that changes are valid and appear instantaneous. We can, however, still shoot ourselves in the foot with sloppy thinking.

It's difficult to demonstrate the complexities of state management in the kind of toy code that festoons documentation, blog posts, and yes, even books like this one. It helps to keep a few guidelines in mind when applying the mechanisms we've seen in action.

How and When to Validate

Our shopping.store API contains a piece of redundancy and a little bit of nastiness. In init, we applied the no-negative-values? function to our inventory as a validator function to safeguard against code that ignores our API (specifically grab) and updates the store's inventory directly.

Our validator method inspects *every element of the map* to verify that the inventory is on the up and up—probably not a good idea. What happens if inventory starts to get large? How much overhead would that be compared to the in-stock? test we use in grab? In addition to being nasty, it's redundant: the validator is called whether we use grab or not.

What to do? At the very least, we should add ^{:private true} to our def of inventory, encouraging the use of grab. A more robust solution is to construct a function that initializes the system and pass that around to the components that require it. This is a toe in the waters of *composition*, which we talk about in more detail in *Compose Your Application*.

When developing your API, try to provide a set of functions that wrap every action you're likely to want, and make the actual data storage private. This prevents bypassing of the provided functions and operating on the data directly. This, in turn, allows us to put mechanisms in place that guard against shenanigans on occasions when a validator would perform poorly. Remember that validator functions execute *before* Clojure commits the transaction, so a long-running validator can either block or queue up requests for your stateful resource.

On the other hand, defining a validator function works great for small pieces of data or program state. If (for example) you have an atom containing configuration that includes a filename for logging, you might want your validator to ensure that the file exists. If you have many types of updates possible on an atom, using a validator can centralize your validation and cut down on the amount of code you need. Of course, then you have to be ready to catch the ensuing exception when someone breaks the rules, but design will always be about trade-offs.

Runtime State vs. Program State

Rest assured, this is a hair worth splitting. In this chapter, we've been talking mostly about *program state* or application state. That is, we've been concerning ourselves with managed state that rests in the problem domain, with inventories and shopping lists and such. Program state serves to provide managed access to data and concepts that are directly related to the domain knowledge that your software models, and the problems that software attempts to solve.

Our store API contained an inventory atom to which we added a sold-items atom later. Our family shopping trip managed a shopping list, assignments, and shopping cart. All of these elements are program state. Program state should be accessed using APIs where possible, to be used through carefully curated methods rather than directly.

Runtime state, on the other hand, exists to facilitate the software's execution. Runtime state serves to keep references, perhaps to databases, config files, network connections, or components we intend to call. They affect the operating environment and aren't concerned with the domain information. We'll explore runtime state in more detail in *Compose Your Application*. Runtime state is often unavoidable, and it's difficult to minimize without compromising configurability. If you're looking to cut down on the amount of state information your software requires, look instead in the program state.

When you're new to functional programming, your reflexes tend to litter the domain with all sorts of unnecessary mutability. You can attack this tendency from two directions: first, watch for it up front; second, pare down your mutability at the end.

Keeping a Leash on Change

You can squeeze the most power out of Clojure when you adhere closely to its core principles. When managing change, you want to *build just enough* to ensure that the application's needs are met. The process we've outlined so far will naturally limit the development of program state until we shift our focus from the problem domain and its entities and transformations to the application domain, continuity, and interaction between components. You should be as follows along your application's development path.

You've constructed entities that are immutable values. They depend on nothing that's stateful, only their own domain values. Complex entities can contain simpler entities, but they're still only values.

Your transformations are pure functions. They take in values and emit values. Those that transform collections take those collections as arguments and return new collections. As functionality begins to span multiple domains, you've ensured that values—not program state—are your stock in trade.

Only after these things have been settled is program state necessary; you're writing your transaction management functionality later rather than sooner. The need for managed change has been limited by good development practice. Now, though, you're creeping into application-level concerns—connecting the language and function of the domain to the users of the system—and program state is required.

It's hard to say how much application state is too much. Rather than figuring out an inaccurate abstract measure in terms of the number of refs, vars, and so on, keep the following truth firmly in the front of your mind when designing software with Clojure: every side effect and mutable reference slows you down.

Wrapping Up

When building an application, we often find ourselves carrying updates forward through an otherwise pure application. If we're clear about the rules, are responsible with our functions, and make good choices about what we need to manage, we can do it effectively.

Viewing your data and its changing state as a series of snapshots allows you to act responsibly when considering the presence of observers in other processes. In Clojure, those snapshots are kept as previous versions wrapped up in mutable references. This ensures that all observers have a consistent set of values as of a particular instant, and no one finds themselves in unfortunate circumstances.

We started this chapter by exploring the ideas about identity and state in terms of time. Using those ideas, you learned about Clojure's facilities for global state with vars, and managing updates using atoms and refs. All these things help us keep our stories straight over time. You now have the tools to move forward into concurrency.

In the next chapter, we'll begin looking at (and thinking about) concurrent processing. We'll also be taking a deeper look at core.async, which we saw when shopping with our kids. Agents will round out our managed roster.

## CHAPTER 5

Use Your Cores

Servers, laptops, and even phones these days are built on multicore chips with multiple independent threads of control available for programs to use. We need to design our programs to take full advantage of these chips. Clojure was born in and designed for this multicore world.

Most of the problems with concurrency in languages like Java are problems of managing shared mutable state. As we've seen, Clojure relies primarily on immutable data (which can be safely used across threads). We've also seen how explicit state can be created using the stateful containers (atoms, refs, agents, and vars). All of these containers use a common *update model* whereby state is always transformed from one immutable value to another with a pure function. The combination of these approaches removes many common classes of error, allowing us to focus on the real problem of how to get all those cores doing something useful.

One of the first problems we encounter is how to move work off the main thread and perform it asynchronously while the main thread goes about its business. Once we do that, we also need a way to receive results from those asynchronous tasks when they're done. We'll dive into Clojure's future and promise for these.

For longer-lived *task-oriented* concurrency, we'll process a series of tasks by farming them out to a pool of worker threads. Java has robust tools for queues and workers that we can invoke directly from Clojure. These tools allow us to efficiently process streams of work while utilizing all of our cores.

In some cases, we need to implement fine-grained work, in parallel, over collections, performing the same transformation on every element. We've already seen how to approach these problems with collection and sequence functions, but Clojure has another option called reducers. Reducers allow us to compose transformations as if they were sequences but execute them in parallel.

Finally, we want to consider how we can use threads (and lightweight processes) to organize the overall structure of a program. The core.async library defines the concepts of *channels* and *go blocks* to help us with this organization. We'll see how to define the application structure.

Push Waiting to the Background

Most programs connect to the external world through files, sockets, or standard terminal streams. We call all of these input/output or I/O. Modern processors can perform billions of instructions per second, but most I/O is comparatively slow. Many programs spend substantial amounts of time waiting to read data from files, receive responses from external servers, or find out what the user wants to do.

We need to do this waiting efficiently so that our programs can continue working on other things. While we're waiting we can either perform other processing or wait for multiple things in parallel. For example, your web browser is a program that spends time waiting for external web servers to return content, while simultaneously rendering the current page and responding to a user clicking links and scrolling around the page.

Fire and Forget

Let's first consider the simple case of work that needs to be done in the background, with no response necessary. Imagine that we're building an application and want to call an external metric collector every time an event happens. We can wrap our external service in a helpful function called inc-stat. We invoke it with the stat to update:

```
(inc-stat :pageview)
```

This function is going to call an external web service over the network. If we call it while producing our page view, the time to make that call will slow down building every page, as you can see in the following figure.

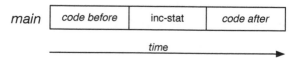

To move this work onto a background thread, we use the future function included in Clojure:

```
(future (inc-stat :pageview))
```

The future function takes a body and invokes that body on a background thread pool maintained by Clojure itself. We can see the difference in the figure:

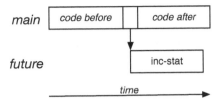

You can also use future-call to asynchronously invoke a no-argument function instead of passing in a body. Either function returns a java.lang.Future object that can be used to control and inspect the asynchronous activity. The future-cancel function will cancel its execution, whereas future-done? and future-cancelled? will give us information about its status.

However, it seems inefficient to be sending a flood of independent statistic-increment messages to the remote service. It would make more sense to batch up a few increment messages before sending. To do that, we need to be both asynchronous and stateful.

Asynchronous and Stateful

In *State, Identity, and Change* we examined several state containers in Clojure: vars, atoms, and refs. We delayed the introduction of one more state container —*agents*—until now.

Like the other state containers, agents hold an immutable value and are modified using the same update model. Unlike the other containers, agents are updated asynchronously.

Consider our metrics collector. Let's hold the counter for a particular statistic in an agent:

cljapplied/src/ch5/stats.clj
```
(def pageview-stat (agent 0))
```

Rather than calling the remote service on every agent update, we'll call it only on every tenth update (when the agent's state reaches a count divisible by 10). This is easy to do with a watch (which works on all the state containers):

cljapplied/src/ch5/stats.clj
```
(add-watch
  pageview-stat
  :pageview
  (fn [key agent old new]
    (when (zero? (mod new 10))
      (remote-send key new))))
```

Here we added a watch to the pageview-stat agent that will be fired with any change to its state. Now we'll the fire external service request only when the new agent's state is a multiple of 10, which gives us some batching.

We can then define the increment function our application will use as just a function sent to be executed asynchronously on the agent:

cljapplied/src/ch5/stats.clj
```
(defn inc-stat [stat]
  (send-off stat inc))
```

Clojure provides two functions for asynchronously invoking update actions on an agent: send and send-off. Use send for agent updates that are computational and won't block for I/O. The underlying thread pool uses a fixed set of threads and relies on these updates completing in a timely manner. Use send-off for updates that might block for an arbitrary time. The underlying thread pool (also used for futures) will grow as needed, so blocking isn't an issue. In inc-stat we are potentially invoking an external service (via watches, which execute in the agent thread), so we use send-off.

One additional feature of agents is that any send or send-off invoked on an agent inside an STM transaction or inside an agent action itself is delayed until the transaction completes. This makes agents safe to call from within an STM transaction (which may have to retry to succeed) or within another agent's update action to produce a side effect.

Shutting Down

In Java, threads can be marked as *daemon threads*. The JVM shuts down gracefully when all nondaemon threads have completed their work (typically this happens when the main starting thread completes). Marking a thread as a daemon thread means that it's a background worker and shouldn't prevent shutdown.

The threads that process futures and agent actions are *not* daemon threads. If you find your application hanging instead of exiting as you expect, you likely need to add a call to shutdown-agents during application exit.

So far, we've been performing actions that block in the background, without using any response. Let's look at how we can receive responses from work done on a background thread.

Waiting for a Response

Sometimes we want to push work to the background but come back later to pick up the result. For example, consider an application in which we want to take a product and look up the price on two (or more) online stores. We could query each store in order on a single thread, like this:

cljapplied/src/ch5/stores.clj

```
(defn query-stores [product stores]
  (for [store stores]
    (query store product)))
```

The time to execute this will be the sum of the times to query each store, as we see in the following figure.

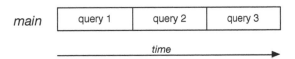

We can do better! With our magical ability to push work onto a background thread, we can query all those stores at the same time. We'll use a future for each asynchronous query:

cljapplied/src/ch5/stores.clj

```
(defn query-stores [product stores]
  (for [store stores]
    (future (query store product))))
```

However, as we mentioned, calling future returns a java.lang.Future object—so query-stores now returns a sequence of those, rather than the actual results. To block and wait for the result of the asynchronous call, we need to dereference the Future with deref or the shorthand, @.

We implement our query-stores function in two stages. The first stage (which we already have) launches all the queries and produces a sequence of Future objects. The only change we need to make is to force that launching to happen eagerly—not lazily—by calling doall. If we don't call doall, the queries won't be launched until the sequence is realized later. The second stage dereferences each of the Futures, blocking until each completes:

cljapplied/src/ch5/stores.clj

```
(defn query-stores [product stores]
  (let [futures (doall
                  (for [store stores]
                    (future (query store product))))]
    (map deref futures)))
```

The query-stores function returns a lazy sequence of results from each store. We could also return the lazy sequence of futures without dereferencing them. The caller would then have full control of when to block to resolve each result.

Now that we're executing our queries concurrently, we can wait for several services at the same time, reducing the overall time by leveraging more threads, as shown in the following figure. The figure shows three query-stores being invoked on futures, then waiting to dereference the results of each query.

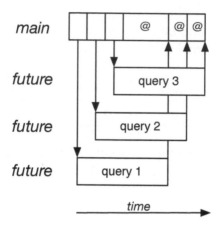

Using futures in this way has one downside: the asynchronous computation can only return a single result back to the original code. If we want to return multiple values at different points in the computation, we can use a promise.

Making Promises

A promise is used to transfer one value (and only one!) from one thread to another. Multiple promises can thus be used to return values at different times in an asynchronous computation. For example, suppose we want to time an asynchronous computation and later get the beginning and ending times for its execution:

cljapplied/src/ch5/stores.clj

```
(defn launch-timed []
  (let [begin-promise (promise)
        end-promise (promise)]
    (future (deliver begin-promise (System/currentTimeMillis))
      (long-running-task)
      (deliver end-promise (System/currentTimeMillis)))
    (println "task begin at" @begin-promise)
    (println "task end at" @end-promise)))
```

In this example we create two promises, begin-promise and end-promise. Values are delivered through a promise with the deliver function. Values can be delivered through a promise only once; after the first delivery, subsequent deliveries have no effect.

Each of these promises can be dereferenced later to retrieve the value. This dereferencing will block until a value is available, then return it. To see if a promise's value is available without blocking, use the realized? function. Also note that a variant of deref will wait for a specified timeout period.

We can use futures and agents to do work asynchronously, allowing us to push waiting or work onto background threads. Futures and promises allow us to control how we can return results from those asynchronous tasks as well. We need to look at how to structure our programs to perform the real work (whatever that may be for you).

Queues and Workers

Many programs can be seen in whole or in part as *task processors*, where a *task* is a unit of work usually mapping to an external request. A web app receives requests to build web pages. A web service receives requests to process API calls. A batch program reads files from disk or a database and processes each one appropriately. All of these common patterns can be modeled as a queue of work farmed out to a pool of workers.

The queue orders and holds the tasks, decoupling the place where work arrives from where it's processed. The worker pool allows us to create pools of workers with different properties, controlling the amount of concurrency and policies used in managing and monitoring the work. That control allows us to make full use of the hardware at our disposal.

Clojure provides some tools for queues and workers but also avoids reinventing the high-quality tools already available in Java. Let's consider how we could create a queue and worker pool from parts we've already seen in Clojure.

Some Assembly Required

In *Model Your Domain* we used Clojure's persistent queue to provide more efficient access than lists or vectors for FIFO data. However, we did so in the context of a single thread. In the persistent queue, every modification of the queue returns an updated version. If more than one thread shares the queue, they all need to share the same instance. We need either a state-management construct (such as an atom or a ref) or a stateful queue implementation.

One option would be to wrap a persistent queue into a Clojure atom or reference such that both ends of the queue maintain a stable identity. If you attempt to do this with atoms you'll find that the atom swap! function can only return the new value of the atom (a queue for us) and not the popped value. This makes it difficult to pull items from this kind of queue in a stateful way.

The ref option looks more promising. We could implement it like this:

cljapplied/src/ch5/queue.clj
```
(defn queue
  "Create a new stateful queue"
  []
  (ref clojure.lang.PersistentQueue/EMPTY))

(defn enq
  "Enqueue item in q"
  [q item]
  (dosync
    (alter q conj item)))

(defn deq
  "Dequeue item from q (nil if none)"
  [q]
  (dosync
    (let [item (peek @q)]
      (alter q pop)
      item)))
```

However, this queue doesn't block! We typically want the consumer to block in deq when the queue is empty waiting for data to arrive, but this implementation will just return nil and would instead require the consumer to poll repeatedly. For this reason, Clojure's persistent queue is usually not a good tool for managing a queue of work across threads.

Instead, we need to look at Java's support for queues and workers. This is an area where the Java library has strong support for a wide variety of behavior.

Java Queues

Most of the Java classes that support queues and workers can be found in the java.util.concurrent package. Java provides many blocking queue implementations (all implementations of java.util.concurrent.BlockingQueue), and they can easily be used from Clojure.

One of the main differences among the Java queue implementations is in how they buffer data. For example, LinkedBlockingQueue provides an optionally bounded buffer, ArrayBlockingQueue provides a bounded buffer, and SynchronousQueue provides no buffer at all—the producer and consumer must wait until both are ready to hand a value from one to the other. LinkedTransferQueue combines the hand-off capabilities of SynchronousQueue with an optionally bounded buffer.

All of the queues we've mentioned so far provide values in a FIFO order, but Java also provides two queues that reorder items. PriorityBlockingQueue bubbles high-priority items to the front of the queue. The DelayQueue takes messages with a delay and only makes them available as delays expire.

Bounded buffer queues also offer an opportunity for customization when a producer encounters a full buffer. The Java blocking queue API allows for blocking, timed blocking, returning a special value, or throwing an exception.

You can call put, take, or other BlockingQueue methods through normal Java interop method calls. Let's push some messages through a queue:

cljapplied/src/ch5/jqueue.clj
```
(ns ch5.jqueue
  (:import [java.util.concurrent LinkedBlockingQueue]))

(defn pusher [q n]
  (loop [i 0]
    (when (< i n)
      (.put q i)
      (recur (inc i))))
  (.put q :END))

(defn popper [q]
  (loop [items []]
    (let [item (.take q)]
      (if (= item :END)
        items
        (recur (conj items item))))))

(defn flow [n]
  (let [q (LinkedBlockingQueue.)
        consumer (future (popper q))
        begin (System/currentTimeMillis)
        producer (future (pusher q n))
        received @consumer
        end (System/currentTimeMillis)]
    (println "Received:" (count received) "in" (- end begin) "ms")))
```

The pusher function pushes n numbers onto a queue, followed by a final :END message to signal completion. The popper function pulls messages off the same queue until the :END message is received. We run both of these functions in futures that will be executed on the background thread pool.

We don't control which thread runs those futures, though. Clojure's futures and agents provide a relatively simple API for asynchronous execution, but there's some loss of monitoring and control. Instead we can use Java's built-in support for running work over many threads.

Making Threads

Java provides interfaces to represent a factory for threads (ThreadFactory) and a combination queue + worker pool (ExecutorService).

You can create a fixed pool of computation threads sized to your processor count like this:

```
(import '[java.util.concurrent Executors])
(def processors (.availableProcessors (Runtime/getRuntime)))
(defonce executor (Executors/newFixedThreadPool processors))

(defn submit-task [^Runnable task]
  (.submit executor task))
```

Java represents a runnable task using the Runnable or Callable interfaces. Helpfully, every Clojure no-argument function implements these interfaces. A task (any Clojure function) can be passed to an ExecutorService for invocation. So it's easy to tap into a stream of requests and submit those as tasks for execution.

Java executors, added in Java 5, were designed to support coarse-grained task parallelism for the four- to eight-core machines common at the time. As machines added cores, the contention caused by waiting on a single queue created a bottleneck for workers retrieving items from the queue.

To address this and take advantage of other computation patterns, Java 7 introduced a new framework called *fork/join*. Fork/join is designed and tuned to support smaller fine-grained computational tasks, recursive computation, and a higher number of cores. Fork/join uses many worker queues and allows them to "steal" work from one another. That is, if a queue runs out of work to do, it takes tasks from the back of another queue, automatically balancing the work across queues.

The java.util.concurrent.ForkJoinPool class is the main entry point for Java's fork/join implementation. Once you construct a ForkJoinPool, it's also an ExecutorService and you can submit tasks to it in the same way. However, Clojure provides a framework that leverages fork/join in ways more natural to Clojure developers. Next we'll look at how and when to use that framework.

Parallelism with Reducers

Most data manipulation in Clojure is specified in terms of functions applied over sequences. Sequences (by their definition) are logical lists of values in some order. Most of the core library sequence functions are applied lazily, in order, and on a single thread. As you might guess in a chapter about using your cores, that last detail is a problem.

Reducers are an alternative way to express transformations over sequential data and feel similar to sequence function composition. However, reducers can execute those transformations in parallel using fork/join.

From Sequences to Reducers

Let's consider a concrete example. A shipping company has data about all of the products that it needs to ship right now. Each product is a domain entity and has keys for shipping class and weight (among other attributes):

```
{:id "230984234"
 :class :ground
 :weight 10
 :volume 300}
```

To calculate the total weight of all current ground shipments, we can use our sequence functions to select only the ground shipments, extract their weights, and add them together:

```
shipping/src/shipping/domain.clj
(defn ground? [product]
  (= :ground (:class product)))
```

```
shipping/src/shipping/seq.clj
(defn ground-weight [products]
  (->> products
       (filter ground?)
       (map :weight)
       (reduce +)))
```

Clojure makes it easy to express our program as a series of composable operations on sequences. Laziness, supported by optimizations like chunking and transients, makes it possible to run these operations efficiently on large product lists. However, this code will only use a single thread to do the work.

Clojure provides a special parallel version of map called pmap, which takes elements of a sequence and performs their work in parallel by sending different elements to background threads with future.

However, in most cases the task to be done per element is small (here, just extracting one attribute from a map). Calling future adds synchronization overhead to pass the work across a thread boundary and pull the result back. When the task is small in comparison to this overhead, pmap can be slower than its single-threaded counterpart. Additionally, in this use case we still haven't made the filter or reduce parts of the code parallel.

Clojure has a solution to this problem: reducers. Reducers provide a way to structure our data transformation as a series of composable fine-grained operations (just as we do with sequences) but achieve parallelism while executing the entire transformation. As a bonus, reducers avoid creating most of the intermediate results we see with sequences (which later must be reclaimed by garbage collection).

A reducer consists of a *reducible collection* combined with a *reducing function*. A reducible collection is nothing more than a collection that knows how to perform a reduce operation on itself as efficiently as possible. The reducing function is a function describing how to accumulate a result during a reduce (just like the function we normally pass to reduce).

A number of reducer operations are provided that mirror the versions we already use in the sequence library (map, filter, mapcat, and so on). Each of these operations takes and returns a reducer but doesn't perform the transformation. Instead, these operations merely modify the reducing function to take the new operation into account.

To perform the transformation, we invoke a new reduce-like function called fold. As shown in the figure on page 97, fold partitions the source collection into groups, performs a reduce on each group by using the reducing function, then combines the partitions by using a combining function. Currently only persistent vectors and maps can be folded in parallel; all other collections fall back to a single serial reduce. This serial reduce might even be more efficient than the equivalent sequence version because it avoids intermediate results.

Returning to our prior example, we can pull in the clojure.core.reducers library and rewrite our ground-weight calculation using the reducer versions of the functions:

```
shipping/src/shipping/reducer.clj
(ns shipping.reducer
  (:require [shipping.domain :refer (ground?)]
            [clojure.core.reducers :as r]))

(defn ground-weight [products]
  (->> products
       (r/filter ground?)
       (r/map :weight)
       (r/fold +)))
```

This implementation is similar to the original version except it uses functions from the clojure.core.reducers namespace instead of the clojure.core namespace. One of the main benefits of reducers vs. other approaches is that they allow us to retain the composable shape of our operations.

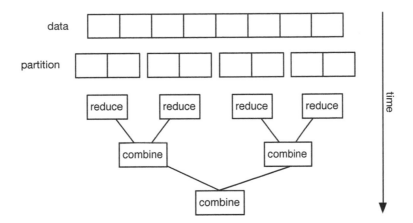

Recall that the reducer versions of filter and map will *not* perform a transformation on the original vector of products! Nothing happens until the final call to fold. In this example, we're using the simplest version of fold, which uses the same function for both the reduce and combine stages.

Any parallel computation that recursively divides a problem needs to decide when dividing and recombining is more expensive than just doing the work. There's no best answer to this—it depends on the size of the individual computations. The fold function allows you to specify the partition size and defaults to 512 elements per group (a sizing that works well with simple arithmetic operations like +). More-complex transformations will likely benefit from a smaller partition size.

We're using reducers to improve our performance on multicore machines, so let's compare the performance between sequences and reducers.

Reducer Performance

We'll run the sequence and reducer versions on increasingly large vectors of products. To understand the details, we'll look at the data at two scales. The following figure shows the results when the number of products (N) is 32, 128, 512, and 2,048. Since the default partition size is 512, when N <= 512, the fold won't actually be parallel; it'll be a single partition. These tests were run on a MacBook Pro with four hyperthreaded cores (reports as eight cores).

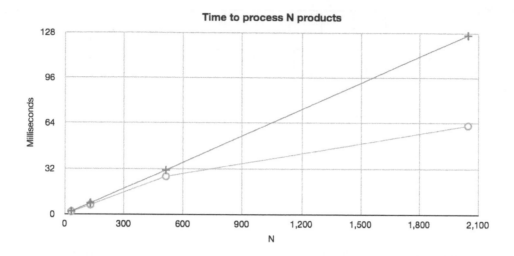

As expected, the performance of the sequence and reducers versions is similar up through N=512. However, once we cross the partition size, the sequence version is single-threaded but the reducer version will split the data into partitions that are executed on different threads in parallel. Let's now pull back and look at the impact on larger values of N by adding three more data points (N=8,192, 32,768, 131,072) in the following figure.

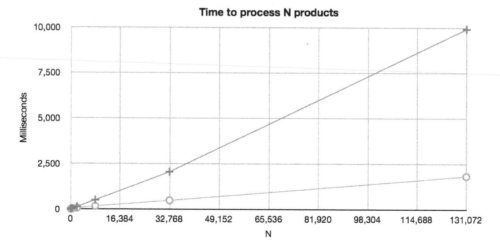

As N gets larger, the benefits of reducers become obvious: reducers are splitting the work across the four available cores, whereas the sequence version is using a single core. Additionally, the reducers version creates less garbage, reducing the load on the garbage collector.

One of the main advantages of reducers is that the same code runs faster when you move to a machine with more cores. We can simulate that by turning off some of our machine's cores to demonstrate the difference. Let's rerun the sequence and reducer versions of the test while fixing N=131,072 and instead varying the number of cores. In this test, we also turn off hyper-threading to eliminate any effects.

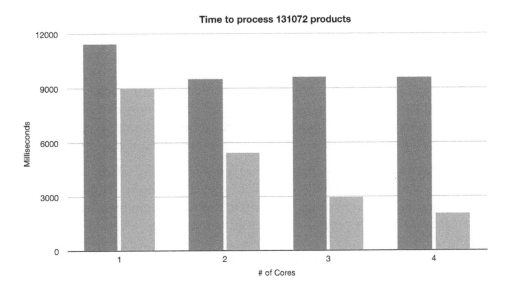

You can see in the preceding figure that the performance of the sequence version is effectively the same regardless of core count, because the code is bound to a single thread anyway. The single-core case is particularly worse because garbage collection and other work on the machine is also using the only core. However, the reducers version clearly benefits from the extra cores, and the same code automatically gets faster. We can extrapolate that moving to an 8- or 16-core server would make this code faster yet.

When you use reducers, it's important to think about the size of your data, the size of the work per partition, and the number of cores you expect to have. When the number of elements is less than the partition size, you'll be single-threaded (but you still might see mild benefits). Once you cross the partition size, your reducer will be multithreaded, but due to the overhead the benefits will likely not be a multiple equal to the number of cores.

Another key is that the only parallel foldable collections (right now—more might be added) are persistent vectors and persistent maps. All other collections (and sequences) will fall back to a reduce over a single partition. It's likely that that reduce will be faster, but it won't be multithreaded.

Reducers combine the benefits of the sequence library's ease of use with the multithreaded performance of fork/join—the best of both worlds. To make the most of reducers, limit their use to cases where the amount of processing is substantial and the data exists in foldable vectors and maps.

Thinking in Processes

Until now you've seen how to use cores for one-time asynchrony (futures and promises), coarse-grained task parallelism, and fine-grained data parallelism. Sometimes, though, we're interested in concurrency rather than parallelism —that is, the ability to design our program as a set of concurrent threads of execution. Inevitably, we'll also want to convey values between these threads of execution, not just a single time but as a series of values over time.

The core.async library was created as an answer to these needs. It was originally conceived as part of Clojure itself but was ultimately released as an independent library to allow for more-rapid evolution than the core language. The core.async library provides two central concepts: *go blocks* (independent threads of execution) and *channels* (a means of passing values from one place to another). We'll explore how to use these next.

Channels

Channels are a queue-like means of conveying a series of values between two or more parts of the program over time. Channels can be created and passed around between threads—they're stateful.

Channels use a buffer to hold values within the channel. By default channels are unbuffered (zero length), similar to a Java SynchronousQueue. Unbuffered channels block until both a producer and a consumer are available to hand a value across the channel. The core.async library also provides fixed-length buffers, dropping buffers (drop new data if full), and sliding buffers (drop old data if full).

To create a channel with core.async, use the chan function. Here are some examples of creating channels with different buffer types and sizes:

```
(require '[clojure.core.async :refer (chan dropping-buffer sliding-buffer)])

(chan)                    ;; unbuffered (length=0)
(chan 10)                 ;; buffered (length=10)
(chan (dropping-buffer 10)) ;; drop new values when full
(chan (sliding-buffer 10))  ;; drop old values when full
```

Any typical Clojure value can be placed in a channel and will be conveyed to the other side. The one exception is nil, which is a special value used to indicate that a channel has been closed and no more data remains. Channels are closed with the close! function.

The two most important operations on a channel are *put* and *take*, each of which has several forms depending on context and use. When using channels from ordinary threads, the put operator is >!! and the take operator is <!!. Here's an example that creates a channel, puts a value into it, and takes it back out:

```
(require '[clojure.core.async :refer (chan <!! >!!)])

(def c (chan 1))
(>!! c "hello")
(println (<!! c))
```

In the preceding code example we're doing both the put and take operations from our current thread, but in a real program the two ends of the channel are typically being used from different threads or components to send values between them. You might also notice that we created a channel with a buffer of size 1. If we had used an unbuffered channel, the put would have blocked waiting in this example, preventing the example from completing.

Channels in core.async are never unbounded. This is an intentional design constraint to avoid architectural problems that will cause you trouble later. Unbounded queues in your system are places where unexpected load will pile up, eventually exhausting resources and crashing your system.

Instead, core.async requires you to bound the length of your buffers by choosing a fixed size or instantiating a policy for what to drop when they're full. Fixed-size buffers create *backpressure* by making producers block when trying to add to a queue that's full. This encourages design thinking up front, rather than in production: your system must be designed to explicitly deal with the block by waiting for the load to clear, accepting less work, or choosing which work not to do.

Although it's possible to use channels entirely from dedicated threads in different subsystems, it's more common to use them from go blocks. Go blocks allow you to create lightweight processing loops that can be supported by a pool of threads.

Go Blocks

Traditionally, Java (or Clojure) programs create threads (which map to real operating-system threads) to contain the actual processing for each part of the program. The core.async library follows a different tradition, based on the heritage of C. A. R. Hoare's classic work on *Communicating Sequential Processes (CSP) [Hoa78]*.[1]

We won't dive into the details of that work. The important thing is learning to think in a different way about how we structure programs. Threads are scarce and expensive resources. They consume stack space and other resources, and they're comparatively slow to start. When these threads block for I/O, we waste those system resources.

Instead, core.async encourages us to think in terms of lightweight processes that are mapped to a thread pool and run only when work is ready to be done. Instead of blocking while waiting for messages to go in or out on channels, those processes can be *parked* until the process is ready to run again. This allows us to run processes only when there's work to do. Also, it allows us to implement some interesting new behavior for *selecting* across multiple I/O operations and proceeding when the first one completes.

In core.async, we call these processes go blocks (in a nod to similar concepts in the Go language). Inside go blocks we use channels, though the put and take operations are <! and >!.

Here's an example of a function that creates a go block to receive and process messages by printing them:

```
(require '[clojure.core.async :refer (go <!)])

(defn go-print
  "Pull messages from channel c and print them."
  [c]
  (go
    (loop []
      (when-some [val (<! c)]
        (println "Received a message:" val)
        (recur)))))
```

In this example, the go block runs as a lightweight process. When it reaches a channel operation (such as <! or >!), if the channel operation can be performed, execution continues. If the channel operation can't continue, the go block is parked. A parked go block doesn't consume a thread; it's effectively

---

1. http://dl.acm.org/citation.cfm?doid=828.833

a suspended computation waiting for data. When the channel operation can proceed, the go block wakes up for continued execution.

Go blocks are a great tool for breaking up a program into potentially concurrent processes. One use case that core.async supports particularly well with go blocks and channels is building *pipelines* of data transformation stages.

Pipelines

The core.async library provides a family of functions for connecting two channels with a parallel transformation stage: pipeline, pipeline-blocking, and pipeline-async. The pipeline functions move values from input to output channel (similar to the simpler pipe), but provide an important extra feature: parallel transducer execution.

This feature makes pipeline great for creating data transformation stages separated by channels. The parallel execution allows you to fully use your cores while describing the data pipeline in a linear way. Each transducer stage can potentially combine many transformations, so this provides many choices in how parallel to be and where channel separation is worthwhile.

For example, consider a system that processes a stream of social media messages. We could provide a series of transformations defined as transducers:

cljapplied/src/ch5/pipeline.clj
```
;; parse message into set of words
(def parse-words (map #(set (clojure.string/split % #"\s"))))

;; filter messages that contain a word of interest
(def interesting (filter #(contains? % "Clojure")))

;; detect sentiment based on different word lists
(defn match [search-words message-words]
  (count (clojure.set/intersection search-words message-words)))
(def happy (partial match #{"happy" "awesome" "rocks" "amazing"}))
(def sad (partial match #{"sad" "bug" "crash"}))
(def score (map #(hash-map :words %1
                           :happy (happy %1)
                           :sad (sad %1))))
```

These transducers can be composed together in a single-stage pipeline from the incoming stream to the outgoing stream:

cljapplied/src/ch5/pipeline.clj
```
(defn sentiment-stage
  [in out]
  (let [xf (comp parse-words interesting score)]
    (async/pipeline 4 out xf in)))
```

This connects in to out with up to four parallel threads, each processing the combined transducer transformation. However, there might be other analysis that could be occurring in a different pipeline stage while the sentiment analysis is going on, such as logging to an archive. In that case, we can split this stage in two, creating a new intermediate channel before sentiment analysis:

```
cljapplied/src/ch5/pipeline.clj
(defn interesting-stage
  [in intermediate]
  (let [xf (comp parse-words interesting)]
    (async/pipeline 4 intermediate xf in)))

(defn score-stage
  [intermediate out]
  (async/pipeline 1 out score intermediate))

(defn assemble-stages
  [in out]
  (let [intermediate (async/chan 100)]
    (interesting-stage in intermediate)
    (score-stage intermediate out)))
```

We now have a first stage that takes all of the incoming messages and outputs only the interesting ones (using up to four threads) and a second stage that takes the interesting messages and scores them. Due to the lower volume, we can reduce the parallelism to a single thread for the second stage. Once we assemble these stages we also have the opportunity to use the intermediate message channel for other purposes.

Because transducers are composable, they can be stacked together in a single stage or split out across stages. The parallelism of each stage can be varied independently. This is a powerful technique for building efficient data-processing pipelines. Pipelines give up the raw performance of fine-grained data parallelism but yield a more flexible architecture.

Wrapping Up

While we can rely on transistor counts on modern chips to continue increasing in accordance with Moore's Law (for now at least), we can no longer rely on a resulting increase in clock speed. Instead, we should expect an ever-growing number of cores per chip. The future belongs to languages that can automatically leverage more cores as they become available.

We've covered several areas where we can use extra cores to do more work. First we considered performing asynchronous work on a background thread with future. Futures should be your first choice when you need to execute an asynchronous task and possibly communicate back the result. If you need multiple values or delivery from any place in the asynchronous task, use promises. If your asynchronous tasks need to maintain state (for example in a simulation), agents are the best choice for you.

If your system is structured as a queue of incoming work or requests, you should accept that work on a queue and send it to a pool of worker threads for processing. To do so, use tools in the standard Java library to structure your system using queues, threads, and executors.

If your data is sitting in large vectors or maps, you should structure computation to act in parallel on the entire data set using reducers. Reducers give the composability you expect from sequence functions but can fully leverage all cores of the machine and minimize garbage collection by avoiding intermediate objects.

One kind of concurrency that we haven't yet explored is how to break a growing system into pieces. To create long-lived connections between components, we can again leverage core.async. Next we'll focus on how to build those components as we move toward assembling complete applications.

## CHAPTER 6

Creating Components

We've now laid a solid foundation—representing our domain, building aggregate data, transforming data with functions, creating state, and using concurrency. It's time to start building larger units of code that correspond to the problem at hand. We'll call these larger units *components*. Separating our code into components allows us to think at a higher level in pieces that correspond to our problem. Component boundaries are also a good way to divide a code base among multiple developers or teams. They can also be opportunities for reuse.

Components are collections of finer-grained elements (functions, records, protocols) that have a greater overall purpose. They have an external API that callers will use. They also have an internal implementation, often including component state, and can even use concurrency internally to process data in parallel or to create a separate thread of processing to react to events.

We'll start our consideration of components by looking at how to organize the functionality of our application into Clojure namespaces. This applies to all our code, both inside and outside components. Next we'll look at the external API that callers will use. This requires considering both the function-call interface and use of longer-lived core.async channels. Finally, we'll look at how to implement the component internals, managing component state and its life cycle using the tools you've already seen for state and concurrency.

In Chapter 7, *Compose Your Application*, on page 125 we'll be taking these components the next step to full application assembly.

Organizing with Namespaces

Clojure code is compiled and evaluated as a series of individual top-level forms (functions, records, protocols, and so on), but Clojure provides *namespaces* to group those individual forms. Namespaces are named, hierarchical containers that we can use to collect, organize, and name groups of forms. One practical use of namespaces is to allow us to use simple names in our code without worrying that we'll conflict with the same name somewhere else. The namespace provides a means of specifying which one we mean.

Although Clojure code is made up of finer-grained elements, dependencies are declared and loaded at the namespace level, not at the function level. The ns macro in each namespace defines its dependencies, collectively creating a dependency graph. This dependency graph affects the order in which namespaces are loaded. In cases where a namespace provides an implementation of a multimethod or protocol (both open systems for type-specific behavior), this load order can be important, because implementations must be loaded before they can be used.

Both namespaces and components are tools for organization. Namespaces are a language feature for organizing functions, whereas components are a means of organizing at the problem level. These two approaches are both useful and work in tandem to provide structure to our code, ultimately making it easier for other developers to understand and use.

Namespace Categories

We group a set of functions into a namespace in Clojure for many reasons. The following categories can be used to create a logical namespace architecture that reflects the application:

Utility

Utility namespaces provide generic functions organized by domain or purpose. For example, you might create a namespace for string manipulation or parsing a particular file format. Generally, utility namespaces have few dependencies.

Data definition

It's common to define either a custom collection or a set of domain entities in a namespace along with helper functions for using the collection or entities.

Abstraction

Abstractions, like protocols, can be isolated in a namespace with minimal dependencies.

Implementation

On the other side, it's often useful to implement an abstraction defined by a protocol or interface in a namespace. This implementation can then be assembled into an application.

Assembly

Given a set of implementations and a configuration specifying how the implementations should be constructed and connected, an assembly namespace ties everything together. Inside the implementations, generally only the abstractions (protocols) or data structures are used directly.

Entry point

Most applications have one or more entry points that connect the start of the application (which includes the gathering of configuration) to initiate assembly and other life-cycle operations.

The following diagram gives a view of how these kinds of namespaces typically layer together in a library or application.

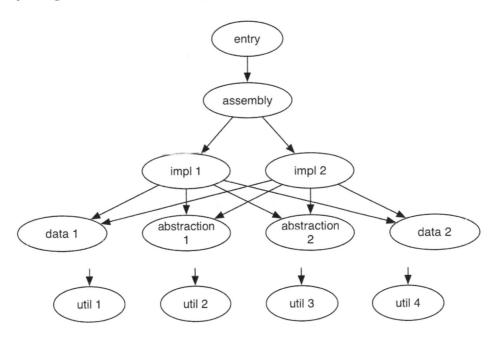

This structure is a useful guideline in designing your own namespace structure. The utility namespaces are at the bottom of the dependency graph, with few or no dependencies of their own and in use by multiple namespaces above. The next layer consists of either data or abstraction namespaces, creating the building blocks for the application itself. Above the abstractions are the implementations of those abstractions. Above those you'll find an assembly layer where configuration is processed, implementations are assembled and connected, and application state is created. At the top are one or more entry points—web apps, command-line interfaces, services, and so on.

You can take many approaches to organizing the namespaces in a project as a namespace tree, with no one right answer. Smaller projects often place the majority of the namespaces within a single root named after the project, with minimal nesting:

```
myproject.util.string   ;; utility
myproject.util.json     ;; utility
myproject.domain        ;; data - domain entities
myproject.config        ;; data - config data
myproject.services      ;; abstraction - service definitions
myproject.impl.xyz      ;; implementation of service abstraction
myproject.assembly      ;; assembly
myproject.main          ;; main entry point - command-line
```

For small systems, it's often easiest to cut services horizontally, grouping many abstractions, implementations, or utilities together. As your system grows, it'll become increasingly useful to break your system into vertical slices, where each particular component can consist of an API, an implementation, a set of data definitions, and utilities.

Public vs. Private Functions

Clojure is biased toward making data and functions available by default. However, most namespaces have functions that are used as helpers or never intended to be part of the public usage. When you're defining the functions in a namespace, consider how a consumer will perceive those functions and is expected to use it. Some tools and conventions are private vars, documentation strings, and the namespace structure itself.

The primary tool built into Clojure is the ability to mark functions as private using defn- or the ^:private meta tag:

```
(defn- internal-function [] ...)
(def ^:private internal-constant 42)
```

Although these vars will be omitted from some namespace function results, they can still be accessed directly with the reader var syntax or by calling directly into the namespace object.

Some documentation-generation tools, such as autodoc, will omit functions that don't have docstrings. Clojure core itself uses this feature to deemphasize internal functions that are useful for advanced Clojure development but not for general use.

Finally, it's common to see namespaces explicitly marked as being internal by using a namespace like myproject.internal.db, where all namespaces under internal are considered nonpublic.

You may find any or all of these techniques useful in indicating to users of your own code where to start.

Now that you have some idea how to organize namespaces, we should use those namespaces to create some components. We'll start by considering how to design the API of components before moving inside to how the components are implemented.

Designing Component APIs

When you identify a component within your application, you should begin by thinking about the purpose it'll serve and how it'll be used by other components. Some typical kinds of components are *information managers, processors,* and *facades.* Information managers track state—either in-memory or in an external data store—providing operations to create, modify, or query that data. Processor components are all about data transformation or computation. Facade components exist primarily to make another external system accessible (and pluggable).

In reality, most components don't fit neatly into these boxes but instead combine one or more aspects into a component that fulfills the unique needs of your own application.

The first thing to consider when designing a component is the API that outside consumers will use. We can interact with components in two primary ways: invoking functions, and passing messages on a queue or channel. Let's look at functions first.

Manipulating Component Data with Functions

API functions are the knobs, buttons, or gauges on our component that allow an external consumer to interact with it. In Clojure, a number of things can be invoked as functions by a user but have different implementations— functions, macros, protocols, and multimethods. (Others—maps, sets, keywords, symbols, and so on—are less useful as part of an API.)

We've raised our focus to the component level, but you need to keep in mind everything you've learned so far. Whenever possible, components should expose immutable data directly. Due to immutability, there's no harm in handing back part of a component's data to the consumer: no copies are required, and the component's own data cannot be affected. Once callers have the data, they're free to use all of the Clojure tools at their disposal in querying or transforming it.

Consider a knowledge-engine component that manages a set of rules used for taking a request and formulating an automated response. Set aside the specific format of the rules for the moment, but assume that each rule is defined as data. We need API functions to add, replace, and delete rules, and a function to find rules based on some criteria. We also need some function to fire the rules and do the job at hand:

```
;; Note: ke refers to the stateful knowledge engine component

;; Read interface
(defn get-rules [ke])
(defn find-rules [ke criteria])

;; Update interface
(defn add-rule [ke rule])
(defn replace-rule [ke old-rule new-rule])
(defn delete-rule [ke rule])

;; Processing interface
(defn fire-rules [ke request])
```

We could then use these functions as follows:

```
(defn example []
  (let [ke (new-ke)]
    (add-rule ke :r1)
    (add-rule ke :r2)
    (add-rule ke :r3)
    (replace-rule ke :r1 :r1b)
    (delete-rule ke :r3)
    (get-rules ke)))
```

However, if we look a little deeper, we can see that a smaller set of functions can support the entire API:

```
;; Get the rule-set
(defn get-rules [ke])

;; Transform from one rule-set to another
(defn transform-rules [ke update-fn])

;; Produce a response from a request
(defn fire-rules [ke request])
```

The find-rules function can be implemented as a filter over get-rules. The add-rule, replace-rule, and delete-rule functions can all be seen as an application of transform-rules on the full rule set.

Most APIs have this pattern—a handful of key base functions and a larger set of functions provided for ease of use. Protocols are a good way to capture the core set of functions so that multiple implementations can extend that protocol. The derived functions should be provided in the API namespace and layered over the protocol. The API functions then work for any entity that extends the protocol.

Putting this all together in a full namespace would look like this:

```
(ns components.ke)

;; SPI protocol

(defprotocol KE
  (get-rules [ke] "Get full rule set")
  (transform-rules [ke update-fn]
    "Apply transformation function to rule set. Return new KE.")
  (fire-rules [ke request]
    "Fire the rules against the request and return a response"))

;; private helper functions

(defn- transform-criteria [criteria]
  ;; ...
  )

;; api fns built over the protocol

(defn find-rules
  [ke criteria]
  (filter (transform-criteria criteria) (get-rules ke)))

(defn add-rule
  [ke rule]
  (transform-rules ke #(conj % rule)))

(defn replace-rule
  [ke old-rule new-rule]
  (transform-rules ke #(-> % (disj old-rule) (conj new-rule))))

(defn delete-rule
  [ke rule]
  (transform-rules ke #(-> % (disj rule))))
```

This implementation defines a component API layered over a small extensible abstraction (the service provider interface), as you can see in the figure.

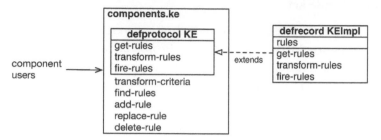

Creating a protocol for the entire API would require any implementation to reimplement all of the functions. Instead, the best tool in Clojure for collecting a set of related functions is the namespace, not the protocol. Protocols are best when we're defining a minimal abstraction for extension, as we do here.

We'll come back to the state-implementation parts of this component later and continue focusing for now on other API considerations, such as asynchronous calls.

Asynchronous APIs

In *Use Your Cores* we've already discussed tools like futures and promises to deliver one-time asynchronous responses for an asynchronous API function. Consider the fire-rules function from the previous section. Producing a response might take a while, so rather than blocking the caller we could also return a future:

```
(let [response-future (fire-rules ke request)]
  ;; ... other work ...
  @response-future) ;; dereference to get the response
```

Returning a future rather than blocking for a response gives callers the choice about when to block (by dereferencing the future). Another option is to accept a callback (to invoke a function) or return a promise (to deliver a result), as shown here:

```
;; send a callback to fire-rules which will be invoked
;; by the knowledge engine
(let [callback (fn [response] ...)]
  (fire-rules ke request callback))

;; send a promise which the knowledge engine will use to
;; deliver the response
(let [result-promise (fire-rules ke request)]
  ;; dereference the result-promise when needed
  @result-promise)
```

Which of these is right for your asynchronous API call depends on the calling code more than the API itself.

Now that we've looked at how to create an API with direct or asynchronous function calls, we also need to consider how to connect components in a more enduring relationship throughout the life of the application.

Connecting Components with Channels

Components may need to be connected to pass an ongoing series of values, feeding them from a producer component to a consumer component. The core.async channels are ideal for this purpose. When a component needs channels for incoming or outgoing values, the component can either accept external channels or create them internally and make them available.

For example, consider a component that receives a stream of incoming social media messages. One option would be to have the component accept the incoming channel as part of its configuration:

```
(defn make-feed-processor
  "Create a new Feed Processor on the given input channel."
  [input-channel] ,,,)
```

Alternatively, the feed-processor can construct the channel itself and allow users to request it:

```
(defn make-feed-processor
  "Create a new Feed Processor"
  []
  (let [ch (async/chan 100)] ,,,))

(defn input-chan
  "Returns the input channel for a feed processor"
  [feed-processor] ,,,)
```

In most cases, accepting external channels creates the most options for assembling your system later, as you'll see in *Compose Your Application*. One of the key decisions that can be made here is the buffering policy for the input channel. If the component creates the input channel internally, it must make this decision. If it needs to be configurable, the component needs to expose buffer-configuration options. If the channel is created externally, the system assembly code is free to configure it along with the rest of the system.

In either case, once we have components with channels, we'll need to connect them in different ways. core.async provides many kinds of channel connectors. We'll break them down in terms of direct connections, fan in, and fan out.

Direct Connections (One-to-One)

Direct connections can be needed when we're combining two components that provide internally constructed channels. To use the two components together, we can connect the channels with a pipe, as in this example:

```
cljapplied/src/ch6/async.clj
(let [component1 (make-comp-1)
      output-chan (get-output component1)
      component2 (make-comp-2)
      input-chan (get-input component2)]
  (pipe output-chan input-chan))
```

Here component1 has an output channel, component2 has an input channel, and a pipe is used to connect them. By default, when the first channel is closed, the second channel will also be closed, effectively combining these two channels into a single channel for producer purposes. The autoclose behavior can be disabled with an optional Boolean flag at the end.

However, from the consuming side, if the consumer closes the second channel, the first will stop consuming input but won't be closed. For long-lived connected components, this difference is likely not important, but it's one difference between a single channel and two channels connected by a pipe. If your components use externally constructed channels, the system can be assembled to directly connect one component to another without the need for an intermediate pipe.

As you saw in *Pipelines*, on page 103, core.async also provides a pipeline function that can be used to link two pipes with a parallel transformation stage.

Fan Out (One-to-Many)

The core.async library makes it easy to publish messages on a channel to many consumers. The most common reason to fan out to is to allow independent consumers to process messages for different purposes (like logging and sentiment analysis in the prior example). The core.async library provides several ways to do this: split, mult, and pub/sub.

The core.async split function takes a single channel and divides the traffic into two output channels based on the truthiness of a predicate. This is shown in the figure.

For example, split is a good way to split invalid messages out of a stream and send them to a separate process for handling.

The core.async mult abstraction takes an input channel and multiplies it onto multiple output channels.

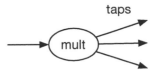

As items are read from the input channel, they're supplied to all of the output channels before moving to the next value. Taps are added to the mult with the tap function (and removed with untap). If a tap is found to be closed, it's removed from the mult.

Because all channels must receive each value, it's possible for one slower tap to hold up the mult. This is where using alternative buffering strategies can be useful. For example, say that you want to tap into the output stream of a particular part of the pipeline to shunt a view to a log, allowing you to peek at what's going on.

This function will connect an input and output channel (similar to what we did with pipe) but also install a logging tap that's returned:

```
cljapplied/src/ch6/async.clj
(defn connect-and-tap
  "Connect input and output and return channel logging
  data flowing between them."
  [input output]
  (let [m (mult input)
        log (chan (dropping-buffer 100))]
    (tap m output)
    (tap m log)
    log))
```

The key thing to see here is that the logging channel is created with a dropping-buffer. If the logging channel isn't keeping up, incoming messages will be dropped. Sadly, we won't see them in the log, but happily our system will continue to stay up and work. This is a good example where the lack of unbounded buffers forces us to think about these scenarios early rather than when the process dies in the middle of the night with a log buffer full of junk.

The mult abstraction provides all messages to all taps. But what if we want a message bus where taps only receive messages appropriate for them? core.async also provides a pub/sub abstraction for exactly this case. The pub function is used to create a published channel with a given topic function. Similar to split, the *topic function* is applied to each message and should return a value, but the value can be anything. The sub function is used to subscribe an output channel to a pub on a topic (the value returned from the topic function).

For example, here's a pub that uses the :topic key (as a function) to look up the topic in each map (or record) message. Two output channels (news-ch and weather-ch) are subscribed on topics :news and :weather respectively:

cljapplied/src/ch6/async.clj
```
(defn assemble-chans []
  (let [in (chan 10)
        p (pub in :topic)
        news-ch (chan 10)
        weather-ch (chan 10)]
    (sub p :news news-ch)
    (sub p :weather weather-ch)
    [in news-ch weather-ch]))
```

When a message contains :news as the :topic, it'll be sent to news-ch. Messages containing :weather as the topic will be sent to weather-ch.

Channels can dynamically subscribe and unsubscribe, making this a capable in-memory message bus.

Now that you've seen ways to take one input channel and fan it out into multiple output channels, let's consider ways to fan in from many inputs to one output.

Fan In (Many-to-One)

In addition to having multiple ways to fan out, core.async has many ways to fan in. merge and mix provide two levels of capability for combining many incoming messages into a single linear output stream.

Consider first the simpler merge, which simply combines all messages arriving on any input channel into a single stream of output messages:

cljapplied/src/ch6/async.clj
```
(defn combine-channels
    [twitter-channel facebook-channel]
  (merge [twitter-channel facebook-channel] 100))
```

The merge is represented in the following figure.

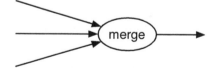

Note that after the collection of channels, you can provide the buffer or fixed-size buffer channel setting for the output channel, as with chan. A merged channel can't be modified after it's created.

When combining many channels, mix acts like an audio mixer, allowing us to control the mix of messages coming from each input and going to the output channel, as shown in the following figure.

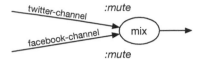

Input channels can be dynamically added with admix and removed with unmix. Each input channel has three toggleable modes:

- :pause—Don't consume input channel or include in output channel.

- :mute—Consume input channel but don't include in output channel.

- :solo—If true, only solo-ed channels are present in the output channel mix (in this case, the pause and mute settings are ignored).

All of these flags can be set on a per-input channel basis via the toggle function:

```
cljapplied/src/ch6/async.clj
(defn mix-channels
      [twitter-channel facebook-channel out]
  (let [m (mix out)]
    (admix m twitter-channel)
    (admix m facebook-channel)
    (toggle m {twitter-channel {:mute true}
               facebook-channel {:mute true}})
    m))
```

This mix was created with both channels muted, meaning that their input is read and dropped without being included.

We can solo one of those channels by setting the solo mode toggle:

```
(toggle m {twitter-channel {:solo true}})
```

In addition to setting toggles on the input channels, it's possible to set the state of the solo mode on the output channel using solo-mode. It can be set to either :mute or :pause, which will mute or pause any solo-ed input channels.

We've now covered all the ways that channels can be connected using the built-in primitives in core.async. In several cases, we highlighted the benefit of having access to both ends of the input and output channels to enable either choosing how to connect (for example, inserting a logging tap), or using the same identical connection without an intermediate process. For both reasons, we recommend that components usually accept channels as part of their configuration rather than create them within the component.

Now that we've looked at how to design the outer surface of a component API, let's consider some finer details of how we implement components.

Implementing Components

Now that we've looked at components from the perspective of how to call and connect them, we need to look inside to how to implement the functionality behind the API.

Most components will hold some kind of state—the component may allow callers to update this state or invoke functionality that depends on it. The state mechanisms you've learned so far (atoms, refs, agents) can be used in many ways, and we'll consider in particular how to choose the granularity of state.

We must also consider the full component life cycle. A component will be constructed with configuration data and dependencies, and it may need to initialize internal state or connections to external systems. Once a component is constructed, it's good to have a path to stop each component as well. This is important for building systems that we can start and stop easily at the REPL during development. We'll look further into both of these.

We'll begin by looking at the granularity of state within each component.

Granularity of State

A component often has runtime state that can change during the life of the component. This may be the data managed by the component, or internal stateful resource handles like database connections, or even dynamic configuration values. Sometimes the initial values for runtime state will be passed as part of configuration, but often it'll be constructed internally or built over time.

When holding state within a component, you'll need to use a stateful container, most likely an atom or a ref. You'll need to choose which to use, and the granularity of state.

The primary decision factor is the level of coordination required. Atoms are simpler but can't coordinate among multiple pieces of state. Refs are more complicated but support coordination. However, here's another way to look at it: it may be possible to bring two pieces of state that require coordination under a single atom, again allowing for a single update function.

Consider a component that needs to manage two kinds of state: an index of accounts and an index of customers. These could be maintained as two atoms:

```
(defrecord CustomerAccounts [accounts customers])
(defn make-customer-accounts []
  (map->CustomerAccounts {:accounts (atom {})
                          :customers (atom {})}))
```

Or if there were cases where changes needed to be made transactionally in both accounts and customers, we could use refs:

```
(defrecord CustomerAccounts [accounts customers])
(defn make-customer-accounts []
  (map->CustomerAccounts {:accounts (ref {})
                          :customers (ref {})}))
```

Using refs requires that we now wrap transactions around any interaction with the component state. We might instead increase the granularity of the state and encompass both accounts and customers within a single atom:

```
(defrecord CustomerAccounts [state])
(defn make-customer-accounts []
  (map->CustomerAccounts (atom {:accounts {}
                                :customers {}})))
```

Because Clojure atoms are fast, it's often possible to use coarse-grained state inside of them, assuming that the update functions are small.

Going the other way, it's also possible to split the granularity of the accounts or customers more finely, for example by splitting accounts by digit or customers by name and creating a ref per segment. The top-level functions of the component will be affected, but data and functions at the entity level should be simple, stateless, and completely reusable for any of these approaches.

Configuration

When you implement a component, it'll need to hold information necessary for startup and ongoing use. A component needs three main kinds of information: configuration, dependencies, and runtime state.

Configuration data will be obtained or constructed outside the component (we'll cover how to manage configuration data in *Compose Your Application*). It's passed into the component at creation time and can be used on component startup or later. One common use of configuration information is connection parameters for external resources (databases, message systems, and so on).

When you construct a component, you could pass each configuration value as a separate parameter:

```
(defn new-component [db-url user password] ...)
```

However, configuration data often varies as a system is developed, so it's better to pass configuration data as a package (a map or record) that can evolve as needed:

```
(defn new-component [{:keys [db-url user password]}] ...)
```

In addition to configuration data, components often need references to other components. For example, a knowledge-engine component may need access to a data-feed component in addition to the config:

```
(defn new-knowledge-engine [config feed] ...)
```

However, rather than passing a component directly to another component as a dependency, in some cases it makes more sense to decouple them by placing a channel between them. In that case, the channel—rather than the remote component—is treated as the dependency. Given all of the ways that components can be connected, this gives a lot of options to the component assembler.

A component needs someplace to store configuration, dependencies on other components or channels, and internal runtime state. Records are the best choice for this because it's common to implement protocols defining component behavior.

Next we'll look at the life cycle of a component, including construction where the component state is created.

Life Cycle

Most components have a simple life cycle. The most important events are construction, component start, and component stop.

For example, consider the rule-based knowledge engine from earlier and how we might construct that component. For the purposes of discussion, we'll also consider that the knowledge engine receives a stream of incoming messages and is responsible for modifying them according to the rules and sending them on to some other components:

```
(defrecord KnowledgeEngine
  [config    ;; map of config info
   ch-in     ;; channel to receive messages
   ch-out    ;; channel to post messages
   rules     ;; state - current rule set
   active]   ;; state - true if active

(defn make-knowledge-engine
  [config ch-in ch-out rule-set]
  (->KnowledgeEngine config ch-in ch-out (atom rule-set) (atom false)))
```

```
(defn start-knowledge-engine
  [{:keys (ch-in ch-out rules active) :as ke}]
  (reset! active true)
  (go-loop [request (<! ch-in)
            response (fire-rules ke request)]
    (>! ch-out response)
    (when @active (recur)))
  ke)

(defn stop-knowledge-engine
  [{:keys (ch-out active) :as ke}]
  (reset! active false)    ;; exit go loop
  (async/close! ch-out)    ;; stop producing
  ke)
```

Because components often need to set up stateful fields with initial values or perform other tasks, you'll usually provide a custom function for creating component instances. Here, the make-knowledge-engine function constructs an instance of the component, including the atom that holds the state of the current rules for the knowledge engine.

Static configuration is often a source of change over the evolution of an application. It's best to plan for this evolution by taking the static configuration as a map rather than as a series of positional configuration parameters. This allows these frequently changing configuration values to vary without breaking existing code, which may simply be passing through values from an external configuration source.

The start-knowledge-engine function activates the component to begin processing the incoming request channel. A lightweight go block is created and will live through the lifetime of the component, extracting a message from ch-in, processing it via the rules, and posting it to the ch-out. The stateful active flag is used to determine whether the go block should continue.

The stop-knowledge-engine function sets the active flag to false, allowing the go block to stop looping. The stop function also closes the output channel, because no more messages will be produced. The input channel isn't closed. Instead, the owner of the incoming channel should be closing that channel when that component is stopped. This is a common convention in core.async programs.

Wrapping Up

Components are a means to build larger units of code that establish the real functionality of an application. Components provide structure and create meaningful subunits of code that teams can use to divide work.

We started with looking at how to design the external API for a component—functions, asynchronous calls, and event streams via channels, as well as how to connect those components using core.async.

We also looked at how to implement each component, taking into account its configuration data, dependencies, internal state, and component life cycle.

Next we'll explore the full picture of assembling systems. You'll see how to manage application configuration data and provide it to components, how to instantiate and connect components, and how to provide system entry points.

## CHAPTER 7

Compose Your Application

In *Creating Components* you learned how to build components, define their APIs, and connect them via core.async channels. Now we'll look at how to assemble those components into actual applications.

We'll start by considering how to take a problem and break it into component-size pieces. Then we'll define the state and API for each component and finally assemble them together into an application.

Each component has its own configuration data. We need to define a strategy for loading configuration from one or more external sources that'll serve us both in development and in various deployment environments. We'll consider two libraries that help with configuration.

Let's start with deciding how to break our problem into components.

Taking Things Apart

Our first task is figuring out how to go from our problem to a rough architecture for solving that problem. We analyze the problem to identify distinct components, which we discussed in *Creating Components*. We separate our code into components for several reasons: reuse of generic components within an application (or across many applications), dividing development within a team, or even a structure that allows us to think about only part of the problem at a time.

Although there are no rules on how to separate components, you can follow some common guidelines. Some reasons to group code together include: the functions work on the same kind of data, the data has a common scope or lifetime, the likelihood of change from external requirements is similar, or the resources needed are similar. If a set of code is reusable when configured differently in more than one context, then it's definitely a useful component.

To make our discussion concrete, let's consider the following problem. Our company needs a system that can monitor and respond to mentions of our products on social media. It's important that those responses be timely, useful, and appropriate. People will be available to serve in this role, but our product is so popular that they need help to automate the process of finding messages that need attention, building candidate responses, and sending those responses.

As we consider this problem, we start to see some boundaries in the application. If we're going to automate the monitoring of social media feeds, we need a component to encapsulate the interaction with each third-party system. These feeds can themselves share many similar implementation needs, even while the interaction with individual systems is distinct. The feeds are distinct components due to their use of an external resource and the coupling of their life cycles to that feed.

Similarly, we'll need a component to encapsulate the knowledge base of rules for how to respond to messages. This can be self-contained or use an external system to invoke the rules.

Finally, there's likely to be some component that takes the original message and the candidate response and presents those to a social media expert to determine whether to approve or modify the message. This component is responsible for handling access to a person.

You can see what the architecture and its high-level components looks like in our sketch on page 127.

Next, let's consider how to define the components we'll need and connect them. As we start to assemble systems, we need to consider the life cycle of the application and components. The best library for these concerns in Clojure is Component.[1] As we define components we'll configure them with start and stop life-cycle functions via Component.

Implementing with Component

For each component, we need to consider the required configuration, runtime state, and connections to other components. Once we've defined our components and their life-cycle methods, we'll see how to assemble the components into a running system.

---

1.   https://github.com/stuartsierra/component

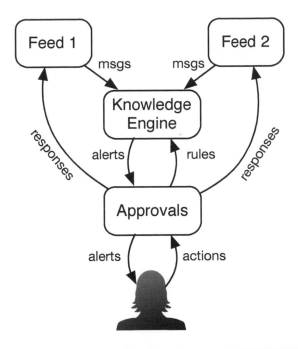

Figure 2—Monitoring Multiple Feeds

Let's start with the social media feeds. Each feed needs authentication config-uration to connect to the feed. Depending on the system, this can be a user-name, password, or other access key. We'll also maintain some runtime state as to whether the feed should be active or paused. Finally, we expect to push new messages on a core.async channel and receive outgoing messages on another channel. We define our component as a record with this information:

```
(defrecord Feed [auth status msg-chan response-chan])

(defn new-feed [auth msg-chan response-chan]
  (->Feed auth (atom :init) msg-chan response-chan))
```

The first auth field contains a map of authentication information specified to the feed type. The status is the changing runtime state (held in an atom). The final two fields are the runtime channels we'll use for outgoing and incoming messages; they're connected on startup and not modified after that.

We now need to extend our feed definition by implementing the component/Life-cycle protocol. First, add Component to the project with the following depen-dency:

social/project.clj
```
[com.stuartsierra/component "0.2.3"]
```

Then add the following require to the namespace:

social/src/social/components/feed.clj
```
[com.stuartsierra.component :as component]
```

And now we can extend the component/Lifecycle protocol, which has just two methods for starting and stopping the component:

social/src/social/components/feed.clj
```
(defrecord Feed [auth status msg-chan response-chan]
  component/Lifecycle
  (start [component]
    (reset! (:status component) :running)
    (process-messages status msg-chan)
    (handle-responses status response-chan)
    component)
  (stop [component]
    (reset! (:status component) :stopped)
    component))
```

The start function does three things: sets the component state to :running, starts a process to stream incoming messages to the msg-chan, and starts a process to handle responses back out to the feed on response-chan. Both of the subprocesses take the status so they can stop themselves when the status changes from :running. Finally, the function returns the same component instance for the rest of startup.

The stop function need only set the status to :stopped. The subprocesses will take care of the rest.

Next let's consider the knowledge-engine component. The knowledge engine will be configured with authentication credentials for an external database of rules and the rule set to use. The runtime state consists of a connection to the external rule database. The component also needs incoming channels from the feed components and an outgoing feed to the approvals component:

social/src/social/components/kengine.clj
```
(defrecord KnowledgeEngine
  [ke-config feed-chan alert-chan rules]

  component/Lifecycle
  (start [component]
    (watch-feeds feed-chan alert-chan)
    component)
  (stop [component]
    component))
```

```
(defn new-knowledge-engine
  "Create a new knowledge engine with no initial rules"
  [ke-config feed-chan alert-chan]
  (->KnowledgeEngine ke-config feed-chan alert-chan
                     (atom (:rule-set ke-config))))
```

The KnowledgeEngine component has a ke-config to hold the component configuration data, the incoming feed-chan, and the outgoing alert-chan. Additionally, this particular implementation has an internal set of rules. That's an implementation detail not exposed in the constructor. Other implementations can manage rules in an external database or rule system.

The knowledge engine's start function sets up a process to watch the incoming feed, process the rules, and if deemed necessary fire an alert message on the alert channel. The stop function doesn't need to do anything special, although we could potentially stop the subprocess.

The knowledge engine has an API that can be invoked directly by the approvals component to manage the rule set. The person approving responses can then also potentially add, modify, or delete rules based on what's coming out of the knowledge engine, ultimately improving the overall system. An example API function for adding a rule is:

social/src/social/components/kengine.clj
```
(defn add-rule
  "Add rule to set"
  [ke rule]
  (swap! (:rules ke) conj rule))
```

Component functions like add-rule are normal functions that typically take the component as the first argument. When the knowledge-engine instance is injected into the approvals component, that component will be able to invoke these functions directly.

Finally, we need to examine the approvals component. This component has some configuration for sending mail to the appropriate people in the case of an alert. It receives incoming messages on the alert channel and forwards them via email or other notification system to the appropriate people. Responses arrive on the response channel and can contain both responses to send back to the feed or new rules to add to the knowledge engine for how to handle this kind of message in the future:

social/src/social/components/approvals.clj
```
(defrecord Approvals [approval-config   ;; approvals config
                      alert-chan        ;; incoming alert messages
                      knowledge-engine  ;; direct hook to knowledge engine
                      response-chan]    ;; output response messages pub/sub
```

```
component/Lifecycle
(start [component]
  (process-alerts alert-chan)
  (process-responses knowledge-engine response-chan)
  component)
(stop [component]
  component))

(defn new-approvals [approval-config alert-chan response-chan]
  (map->Approvals {:approval-config approval-config
                   :alert-chan     alert-chan
                   :response-chan  response-chan}))
```

Note that the Approvals component can assume that Component will properly start and inject the knowledge-engine prior to start being called.

Now that we have all of our components, we need to use a Component *system* to assemble them together.

Putting Things Together

In Component, a system is a special component that can start and stop other components. The components in a system are started in an order such that dependencies are always started before a component. This requires that no cycles are in the component dependency graph. Similarly, when a system is stopped, components are stopped in the reverse order of the start.

A system is defined with the component/system-map function. The map defines a mapping from component name to component instance. When a component has component dependencies, this is specified with component/using, which takes either a vector of injected components (if the names are the same in the system and inside the component) or a mapping from the component name to the system name.

This function creates a Component system map from the components we've defined in our system:

social/src/social/main.clj
```
(defn system [{:keys (twitter facebook knowledge approvals) :as config}]
  (let [twitter-chan (async/chan 100)
        twitter-response-chan (async/chan 10)
        facebook-chan (async/chan 100)
        facebook-response-chan (async/chan 10)
        alert-chan (async/chan 100)
        response-chan (async/chan 100)
        feed-chan (async/merge [twitter-chan facebook-chan])
        response-pub (async/pub response-chan :feed)]
    (async/sub response-pub :twitter twitter-response-chan)
```

```
(async/sub response-pub :facebook facebook-response-chan)

(component/system-map
  :twitter (feed/new-feed twitter twitter-chan twitter-response-chan)
  :facebook (feed/new-feed facebook facebook-chan facebook-response-chan)
  :knowledge-engine
    (kengine/new-knowledge-engine knowledge feed-chan alert-chan)
  :approvals (component/using
                (approvals/new-approvals approvals alert-chan response-chan)
                [:knowledge-engine])))))
```

The beginning portion of the system function creates all of the core.async channels and other channel pipes that are needed for the system. Then the component/system-map function is used to define the four components, how they're configured, and how to inject the knowledge engine into the approvals component. The last part demonstrates a use of component/using with the vector of a single component, which has matching names in the system map and in the approvals component itself.

Each component has some configuration information needed to either start the component or affect its operation. Most applications will have a number of configuration elements. Next, let's look at how to load configuration data in our application in a way that supports the full life cycle from development to deployment.

System Configuration

System configuration contains several kinds of settings: system attributes, per-environment information, and dev-only information. The system attributes are flags or other configuration that affects how your application runs, perhaps turning features on and off or allowing you to externalize magic numbers that may need to change some day. Per-environment information changes for each application deployment target—development, quality assurance, or production. And finally, dev-only settings allow developers to fine-tune an environment on their own machines as they work.

Of these settings, only system attributes can be checked into source control. The per-environment settings should be set outside the application in the environment. The dev-only settings should only be set locally during individual development.

We need to load all of these kinds of values together into one consistent view of the system settings at startup. We'll look at the Environ[2] library as one

---

2.   https://github.com/weavejester/environ

way to get a consistent interface to values obtained from several sources. For a bit deeper solution, we'll instead turn to the Immuconf library.[3]

Environ

The Environ library creates a single view of configuration values pulled from Leiningen profiles, environment variables, and Java system properties. Consider three system-configuration properties we might need: :rule-set (a knowledge-engine rule set to use), :feed1-user (the user name of a social media feed), and :verbose (a debug flag for development time).

At development time, we might want to set the rule-set and feed1-user in our local build. To set this up with Environ, you first need to update your Leiningen project.clj to include Environ as a dependency (for your code) and the lein-environ plugin (for your build):

```
:dependencies [[environ "1.0.0"]]
:plugins [[lein-environ "1.0.0"]]
```

The first place we could set our system-configuration properties is directly inside the project.clj as part of Leiningen profile. Profiles allow you to create bundles of project configuration that are optionally included in your project build. One common use for profiles is to create environment-specific project environments. Leiningen uses a :profiles key containing a map of profile name to profile-specific project configuration:

```
:profiles {:dev  { ,,, }
           :qa   { ,,, }
           :prod { ,,, }}
```

The Environ library expects to read the system configuration from an :env key in the project configuration:

```
:profiles {:dev {:env {:rule-set "basic"}}
           :prod {:env {:rule-set "advanced"}}}
```

The :user and :dev profiles are well-known and on by default in Leiningen, so we can just start our REPL as usual with lein repl to make the dev configuration available:

```
user=> (require '[environ.core :refer (env)])
nil
user=> (env :rule-set)
"basic"
```

---

3.   https://github.com/levand/immuconf

However, the project.clj file is normally tracked in your source control system. While an environment setting like :rule-set is fine, a different configuration setting (like user name and password for your database) is likely unacceptable. In that case, you'll want to store your configuration setting in a separate Leiningen profiles.clj that can be developer-specific and stored outside of source control.

We can modify our example by removing the :profiles from project.clj and putting the value of the :profiles key inside profiles.clj instead:

```
{:dev {:env {:rule-set "basic"}}
 :prod {:env {:rule-set "advanced"}}}
```

The profiles.clj should then be marked as ignored by your source control system. In this way, all developers can specify their own environments without exposing sensitive config.

When you deploy to production, you'll no longer be using Leiningen. Instead you can supply these properties via either JVM system properties or system environment variables:

```
# Invoking your app with Java system properties
java -cp myapp.jar -Drule-set="experimental"

# Invoking your app with environment variables
export rule_set=experimental
java -cp myapp.jar
```

Note that environment variable names can't be created with a hyphen, so an underscore is used instead. Environ translates any property names by replacing underscores and periods with hyphens.

Another key thing to note is that although it's possible to use real Clojure data (like keywords) in your project.clj or profiles.clj file, all values read from system properties or environment variables will be strings. So it's best practice to use only string values as properties to get consistent data independent of your configuration source.

Environ is a simple and effective solution to providing environment-specific configuration, but it has some downsides. First, configuration is expected to be used as a flat map of keywords to strings. As Clojure programmers with access to richer data structures, we'd find it nice to have the ability to create nested maps and use other kinds of Clojure data (keywords, numbers, and so on). Second, for Environ to pick up the profile-based configuration, the lein-environ Leiningen plugin is required. This limits your choices with respect to build tooling and adds an additional plugin requirement.

Immuconf is another library for managing configurations that takes a different approach, sidestepping these concerns and providing some additional functionality.

Immuconf

Rather than build configuration from a variety of property sources, Immuconf focuses instead on specifying a set of configuration files that are combined in a specified order.

Immuconf configuration files are all defined using the Extensible Data Notation (edn) format. This format, which we discuss in more detail in Chapter 9, *Formatting Data*, on page 157, is essentially a subset of Clojure data. Instead of the single flat map of string properties provided by Environ, we can use the full range of Clojure data—most commonly, nested maps.

Let's use Immuconf to accomplish the same configuration we saw with Environ. First we must include Immuconf in our Leiningen project dependencies:

```
[levand/immuconf "0.1.0"]
```

Next we define a configuration file config.edn (any name can be used). It's convenient but not essential to place it in the directory of project resources at resources/config.edn. The contents must be a map defined using edn (Clojure) notation:

```
{:rule-set :basic}
```

Inside our application we can then use the Immuconf API to load the configuration file. In this example we'll store the config in a var, but it's better to store this in the state of the application for use by all application components:

```
(def config (immuconf.config/load "resources/config.edn"))
```

We can then use the Immuconf get function to look up values in the configuration map. The immuconf.config/get function is similar in purpose to clojure.core/get-in. It takes a config map and a series of arguments defining a path into the nested map:

```
(immuconf.config/get config :rule-set)
```

Using Multiple Config Sources

Now we've seen the basics, let's look into how to have project-specific configuration and developer-specific or platform-specific configuration. The load function can accept multiple configuration files, which will be merged from left to right (similar to clojure.core/merge). So we can leave our config.edn file in place and create a new developer-specific user.edn file at the root of our project.

This user.edn file will be a file stored outside source control that provides a dev-specific configuration. For example, if the configuration property were a database URL, it could store a developer's own test database instead of the production database location.

The contents of user.edn would be as follows:

```
{:rule-set :dev}
```

The config can then be loaded with both files instead:

```
(def config (immuconf.config/load "resources/config.edn"
                                  "user.edn"))
WARNING: Value at [:rule-set] in resources/config.edn overridden by
value in user.edn
```

Note that a warning is logged at this point indicating that a value has been overridden. As we expect, invoking get again will return the overridden answer:

```
(immuconf.config/get config :rule-set)
;; :dev
```

Defaults and Overrides

Let's consider again that warning we received when we overrode a value in the first configuration file. In some cases, this is a value we expect to be treated as a default (with no warning); in other cases, we do want a reminder that we're making an unusual modification.

Immuconf allows you to mark default values that are expected to be overridden without a warning with the #immuconf/default tagged literal. In this case we would mark the value in the first config.edn file:

```
{:rule-set #immuconf/default :basic}
```

With this modification, the call to immuconf.config/load won't produce a warning.

Additionally, it's often useful to specify a template of the full config file in your base configuration file and *require* some of the values to be overridden by additional config files. This makes it easier to see the whole picture in a single file that's part of our source. Properties that must be overridden are marked with the #immuconf/override tagged literal and can specify a message that'll appear in an error if the value isn't overridden.

For example, consider a configuration that specifies connection information:

```
{:rule-set #immuconf/default :basic
 :rule-db {:url #immuconf/override "jdbc:db://<host>:4567/dbname"
           :user #immuconf/default "admin"
           :password #immuconf/override "Specify password"}}
```

This configuration adds an additional nested :rule-db configuration element. The URL and password must be overridden for a valid config, and the user has a default value of admin but it can be overridden without a warning.

If we try to load this config without overriding the URL or password we'll see an exception with the following message: Config specified that value at [:rule-db :url] should have been overridden, but it was not. Additionally, the exception is a Clojure ex-info that contains the following data an application could use to format a user exception message:

```
{:override #immuconf.config.Override{:doc "jdbc:db://<host>:4567/dbname"},
 :path [:rule-db :url]}
```

Thus we can use override behavior to fully document what our config file is expected to look like and how to customize it appropriately in a downstream config file.

We've now looked at two configuration libraries that allow you to manage configuration across multiple developer machines and/or platforms. Environ provides a single map of properties that can be loaded from Leiningen profiles, environment variables, or system properties. If your configuration is a simple map of properties and you're using Leiningen, then Environ is a great choice.

Immuconf supports nested maps in edn loaded from a series of configuration files and adds the ability to specify default or required properties. If your system is bigger and more complicated, it's likely that the richer configuration supported by Immuconf will be useful.

Wrapping Up

You now know how to build all the basics of your application. We started with establishing the data of our application, creating domain models, and making the best use of Clojure collections. We then looked at techniques for processing sequential data, working with state, and building concurrent processes. We used all of these tools to create components that function at the business level. Finally, we assembled those components into a full application and saw how to configure it.

Next we'll be looking at a variety of practices that can assist throughout the development effort. The first practice we'll examine is how we test an application and verify its correctness.

Part III

Practices

When you develop in Clojure, your activities include many secondary concerns: testing, connecting to external systems, and deployment. We'll explore common Clojure approaches to these needs.

## CHAPTER 8

Testing Clojure

Programs are written by people. Unfortunately, that means that regardless of how much time we spend planning and designing the perfect program, the resulting code is imperfect. Testing is the verification process that we use to check our work and ensure that our programs do what we intended.

We can take many approaches to testing. Each tool or approach verifies different kinds of problems and has different creation and maintenance costs. As with diversifying a financial portfolio, you must balance the mixture of testing investments in your test suite. Our goal is to maximize the value (in terms of coverage, bugs found, and reduced risk) with respect to the effort (for both initial creation and ongoing maintenance). Generally a mixture of techniques yields the best balance of returns, cost, and risk.

We'll investigate a few of the most common and helpful kinds of testing in typical Clojure applications and some tools used for each one. We'll start with interactive testing in the REPL, which is part of the Clojure development experience itself. After that we'll cover two kinds of unit testing: *example-based* and *property-based* tests.

Interactive REPL Tests

Clojure programmers often work interactively at a REPL to develop functions. The workflow consists of writing a function either in the REPL or in a namespace editor, evaluating that code, and executing that code with sample inputs. Often we visually inspect the results, sometimes saving them so we can perform more detailed checks of their behavior.

The next question is whether the inputs and expected outputs are worth capturing into a test that can run all the time. Some things to consider are:

- Is the test checking business logic or verifying the behavior of chaining together standard Clojure functions? Tests for the logic of your application are almost certainly worth keeping. Simple uses of Clojure itself (say, a function that retrieves a field from a map) probably are not.

- How difficult is it to create the inputs and outputs? One way to capture good input data at the REPL is to capture a variable in the middle of a function (a line you would subsequently remove) before running the whole application. Expected outputs can typically be captured in a similar way from a successful execution of the function.

- How likely is it that the input or output data will change frequently? If the data is changing shape while you work toward the best solution, it may be better to delay capturing and recording this data until those kinds of changes have settled down. In general, complicated inputs and outputs are more likely to change (and this may also be a sign that your data is poorly factored).

- How likely is it that the function under test will change frequently? If the function behavior is changing rapidly, you might want to wait until it stabilizes before recording the test.

- How fast is the test? A fast test cycle has many benefits. If a call is slow, you may not want to include it as a permanent test. Again, this may be a hint that your code needs better factoring.

- Is a test to reproduce a bug worth keeping after you fix the bug? It's virtually always useful to create a failing reproducible test for a bug before fixing it. However, whether you should keep it will depend on the severity of the bug and complexity of the fix.

If you decide that the REPL test should be recorded, you'll need to decide on a way to record the example. The most commonly used framework for this is clojure.test, included with Clojure.

Example-Based Tests with clojure.test

Example-based testing is the process of exercising bits of code by passing known inputs (the examples) and checking that the outputs match expected values. Most Clojure programs are composed primarily of immutable data and pure functions, which are particularly amenable to example-based tests, because no messy mutable state leaks into or out of the code being tested. Example-based testing is most useful when working in the small, at the level of single functions or small groups of functions. This style of testing is most commonly exemplified by the xUnit libraries available in most languages.

clojure.test is a library included in the Clojure standard library that provides facilities comparable to JUnit or other xUnit unit-testing frameworks available in many other languages. Tests are defined with deftest forms that invoke functions and specify assertions about the results.

Let's look at a simple example that tests the Clojure range function. The range function docstring says:

```
([] [end] [start end] [start end step])
Returns a lazy seq of nums from start (inclusive) to end (exclusive),
by step, where start defaults to 0, step to 1, and end to infinity.
```

Starting with the commonly used single-arity form, we'll create a simple test:

cljapplied/src/ch8/test.clj
```
(deftest test-range
  (is (= '(0 1 2 3 4) (range 5))
    "Got 0-indexed sequence when only end specified."))
```

Let's examine the parts of this test:

- Definition: (deftest ...)—The deftest form defines a test named test-range that has a single assertion. The deftest form is really a wrapper around defn that creates a function that takes no arguments. You can think of a test as a function that does nothing but verify that the invocation of functions operate as expected and report what happened.

- Function invocation: (range 5)—We invoke the function we want to test with an example input. When invoked, this will return the actual output.

- Expected output: '(0 1 2 3 4)—The sequence from 0 to 4 is what we expect to be returned from the single-arity version of range.

- Condition: (= '(0 1 2 3 4) (range 5))— The most common condition we'll assert is that the expected output equals the actual output. However, the condition could be any Clojure function call that can be evaluated for truthiness, so there's a lot of freedom to express your intent. There are also some special conditions defined by clojure.test that we'll examine later.

- Message: "Got 0-indexed sequence when only end specified."—If the condition isn't met, we'll report this message to the developer. This message is optional and is frequently omitted in actual test cases.

- Assertion: (is ...)—The is macro evaluates the condition and either continues if true or reports failure using the provided message.

The deftest macro creates a function that we can simply run to run our test at the REPL:

```
user> (use 'ch8.test)
user> (in-ns 'ch8.test)
ch8.test> (test-range)
nil
```

As you can see, merely running the function was less interesting than expected. The test ran and all assertions were successfully verified, so no extra output was generated.

Let's try running the normal clojure.test reporting function to run all tests in the current namespace:

```
ch8.test> (run-tests)

Testing ch8.test

Ran 1 tests containing 1 assertions.
0 failures, 0 errors.
{:test 1, :pass 1, :fail 0, :error 0, :type :summary}
```

That's more reassuring. Let's add some more assertions to see what happens when we ask for an endIndex of 0. Let's check it at the REPL first:

```
ch8.test> (range 0)
()
```

So a range from 0 (inclusive) to 0 (exclusive) yields an empty list. Let's record that example in our test:

```
cljapplied/src/ch8/more.clj
(deftest test-range
  (is (= '(0 1 2 3 4) (range 5))
    "Got 0-indexed sequence when only end specified.")
  (is (= '() (range 0)) "Got empty sequence when end index = 0"))
```

If you run this test, you'll see that it passes. Bouncing among source, REPL, and tests is a common way of working in Clojure.

Those are the absolute basics for writing example-based tests with clojure.test. Often, though, you'll have groups of examples that you want to collect together in your tests.

Grouping Related Examples

If we write tests that are logically related, we can group them with a bit of description using the testing macro:

```
cljapplied/src/ch8/more.clj
(deftest test-range-group
  (testing "Testing range(endIndex)"
    (is (= '(0 1 2 3 4) (range 5))
      "Got 0-indexed sequence when only end specified.")
    (is (= '() (range 0))
      "Got empty sequence when end index = 0")))
```

This serves two purposes. First, we get a visual grouping and summary in the test itself, which might help us understand the test later. Second, these groupings change how a failure is reported. Let's add a failing test and run it:

```
cljapplied/src/ch8/more.clj
(deftest test-range-fail
  (testing "Testing range(endIndex)"
    (is (= '(0 1 2 3 4) (range 5))
      "Got 0-indexed sequence when only end specified.")
    (is (= '() (range 0))
      "Got empty sequence when end index = 0")
    (is (= '(0 1) (range 0)))))
```

As expected, our new test fails and reports the condition that failed in the assertion. Notice also that all of the parent testing context clauses will be printed as well, giving us more context about the failure.

Testing Many Examples

As we start to build out a set of examples to test, you may be thinking that a fair amount of duplication seems to occur in each is assertion. Fortunately, clojure.test has another trick up its sleeve to concisely state a set of examples: the are macro, which has the following form:

```
(are [args] condition & inputs)
```

The args define the input names for the condition, and the inputs consists of a series of values that will be passed into the condition for evaluation. Let's rewrite our previous example with are instead of is:

```
cljapplied/src/ch8/more.clj
(deftest test-range-are
  (testing "Testing range(endIndex)"
    (are [expected endIndex]
      (= expected (range endIndex))
      '(0 1 2 3 4) 5
      '() 0)))
```

Each line following the are defines a set of inputs that are evaluated by the condition. Adding new examples is a matter of adding new pairs of expected output and input. This example has two pieces of data per example, but the assertion definition can be arbitrarily complex, and the are will partition the data based on the size of the parameter list.

Why Is the Expected Value First?

Many xUnit frameworks in other languages use the convention of stating the expected output first. We've followed this convention here, but it's a matter of personal preference; the clojure.test framework doesn't care.

Using are instead of is has two drawbacks:

- The are macro doesn't have support for specifying a failure string for each case.

- Error reporting of line numbers is broken due to getting lost in the are macro, so all errors are reported as occurring on the expression instead of in the failure input data.

Despite these drawbacks, you'll find that are is an essential tool for removing duplication in your example-based tests.

Exceptional Tests

What about testing for expected exceptions? For example, what if we pass a string instead of a number for the endIndex in range? Let's try it first at the REPL:

```
user> (range "boom")
ClassCastException java.lang.String cannot be cast to java.lang.Number
clojure.lang.Numbers.isPos (Numbers.java:96)
```

We can write a test to verify that a ClassCastException is thrown:

```
cljapplied/src/ch8/more.clj
(deftest test-range-exception
  (try
    ;; use doall to force seq realization
    (doall (range "boom"))
    (is nil)
    (catch ClassCastException e
      (is true))
    (catch Throwable t
      (is nil))))
```

Some things to note in this example are:

- Because range creates a lazy sequence, the exception won't be triggered until we force the realization of the range sequence with doall.

- Use (is nil) to force a failed assertion for parts of the control flow that should never be reached.

- Use (is true) to check that part of the control flow has been reached.

This is great, but the test is almost all boilerplate code. Fortunately, the is macro has a set of special conditions that reduce the noise in exception tests:

cljapplied/src/ch8/more.clj
```
(deftest test-range-exception
  (is (thrown? ClassCastException
        (doall (range "boom")))))
```

And you can use a variant for checking the exception message with a regular expression:

cljapplied/src/ch8/more.clj
```
(deftest test-range-exception-msg
  (is (thrown-with-msg? ClassCastException
        #"java.lang.String cannot be cast to java.lang.Number"
        (doall (range "boom")))))
```

Often it's best to use a regular expression that just verifies certain properties of the message (like that it contains a particular word or the invalid value that it's reporting). This makes the test slightly more flexible when your code evolves.

The tests we've shown so far are each isolated tests without any external resources. But we often need to set up external resources or expensive data to run tests that cross parts of the system, and we'll look at that next.

Managing Test Resources

Often all tests in a set of tests need similar resources to be created before the test, and possibly destroyed after the test. One common examples is a connection to an external system like a database. For example, you may have a set of tests with the following form:

cljapplied/src/ch8/fixture.clj
```
(deftest test-setup-db-add-user
  ;; setup
  (let [conn (create-db-conn)]
    (load-test-data conn)
    ;; test logic
    (add-user conn "user")
    (check-user conn "user")
```

```
;; tear down
(destroy-test-data conn)
(close-db-conn conn)))
```

In this test, we have logic at the beginning to set up the test environment and logic at the end to clean it up. This code surrounding the test logic would need to be repeated on every database test.

The clojure.test framework has *fixtures* to address this common need for custom logic before and after a test. A fixture is simply a function that takes the test to invoke. It can then wrap the invocation of the test function with arbitrary custom logic.

The first problem you'll encounter is a need to create a resource (the database connection) and make it available inside the test, since tests are always functions that take no arguments. Dynamic variables are an excellent choice for this: they allow you to create a known variable and then bind it dynamically only in the context of the text execution, so no state hangs around. Additionally, dynamic bindings are per-thread, so tests could safely be run in parallel. Let's rework our example with a fixture:

cljapplied/src/ch8/fixture.clj
```
(def ^:dynamic *conn*)

(defn db-fixture [test-function]
  (binding [*conn* (create-db-conn)]
    (load-test-data *conn*)
    (test-function)
    (destroy-test-data *conn*)
    (close-db-conn *conn*)))

(use-fixtures :each db-fixture)

(deftest test-db-add-user
  (add-user *conn* "user")
  (check-user *conn* "user"))
```

First we create our *conn* dynamic variable. The leading and trailing asterisks are a common naming convention for dynamic variables. The db-fixture function takes the test function to invoke and contains all of the per-test boilerplate.

We install the fixture for this namespace with the clojure.test use-fixtures function. This function can be called either with :each to run these fixtures for each test in the namespace or with :once to run the fixtures only once for this namespace. In both cases, you can pass any number of fixtures, and they'll be invoked in left-to-right order. Only the last use-fixtures of each type will take effect in a namespace; don't call it more than once per type.

Our test function—test-db-add-user—is now much simpler. All setup will be done automatically by the fixture, and we can expect to have *conn* bound when it runs in the test runner. However, this affects our ability to simply run the test as a function, because the fixtures won't be applied outside the test runner. If you know the fixtures that need to be applied, you can manually wrap them before invoking the test:

```
(db-fixture test-db-add-user)
```

The clojure.test framework also has a test-vars function that can test one or more test function vars with the appropriate :each and :once fixtures applied:

```
(test-vars [#'test-db-add-user])
```

Because this style of test definition has effects across an entire test namespace, it's best only to include tests in this namespace that will need use of the fixtures. Other tests should be in a different namespace without the fixtures.

Once you have multiple test namespaces, you need to start managing them and make it easy to run them in the context of your project.

Organizing and Running Your Tests

The most common way to structure Clojure projects is to have two source directories—one for source code and another for tests. Most Clojure tools automatically create and understand projects with this structure.

Tests are commonly stored in a namespace parallel to the namespace being tested, as in this example structure:

```
myproj
├── src
│   └── proj
│       └── util
│           └── string.clj
└── test
    └── proj
        └── util
            └── test_string.clj
```

If we store our string utility functions in the proj.util.string namespace under the src/ directory, the associated tests are stored in a similarly named namespace under the sibling test/ directory. The tests will be available on the classpath when we run tests but will generally not be included in any build output.

Because both the source and the test namespaces will be loaded at test time, we need to name them differently to distinguish them. In this example, we prefixed the final part of the namespace with test-. Some projects instead prefix the beginning of the namespace—test.proj.util.string, for example—or follow other conventions. Use a standard strategy for navigating between source and tests—it helps team members know where to look for the tests associated with any namespace.

To run all of the tests in the test directory with Leiningen, run:

```
lein test
```

You can also run smaller sets of tests instead of the entire suite. To run a single namespace of tests, use this form:

```
lein test proj.util.test-string
```

Leiningen also provides a special test selector to run a single test function without running the entire namespace:

```
lein test :only proj.util.test-string/test-replace
```

Sometimes you'll have a subset of tests across your suite that you like to run together—for example, tests specific to a particular feature or subsystem. In Leiningen, you can mark deftest forms with Clojure metadata and define selectors that run only those tests. First mark a test with metadata:

```
(deftest ^:accounting test-debits ,,,)
```

Then, you must declare your test selector in your project.clj file. The test selectors are a map from selector name (a keyword) to either keyword selectors applied to the test function metadata or specific namespaces. Here we simply need an :accounting selector that finds tests marked with the :accounting metadata:

```
:test-selectors {:accounting :accounting}
```

We can run this with Leiningen as follows:

```
lein test :accounting
```

Additionally, a special :defaulttest selector, if defined, is run instead of all tests. This can be useful when you want the normal lein test command to run less than the full set of tests. For example, performance tests often require benchmarking and can take a while. We want to omit those tests in our normal test runs but create a way to run them when needed. We can define our test selectors as follows in project.clj:

```
:test-selectors {:default (complement :performance)
                 :performance :performance}
```

And then we can run them independently:

```
# Run everything except the performance tests
lein test

# Run only the performance tests
lein test :performance
```

Now that we've taken a thorough look at clojure.test and how to manage and run our tests, let's see a different approach to writing example-based tests and reporting results—with the *expectations* library.

Example-Based Tests with expectations

The expectations library[1] takes the ideas of clojure.test and pushes them further with the goals of simplified test definition and improved feedback. In expectations, every test is a bare form with a single assertion.

For example, rewriting our first clojure.test examples with expectations looks like this:

```
cljapplied/src/ch8/expect.clj
(expect '(0 1 2 3 4) (range 5))
(expect '() (range 0))
```

Each expect at the top-level of the namespace takes an expected value and an expression and checks that the expectation is satisfied.

A number of other special expectations forms test various special cases. For example, passing an exception type will check that the form throws that type:

```
cljapplied/src/ch8/expect.clj
(expect ClassCastException (doall (range "boom")))
```

The expectations library has no built-in check for an exception's message, but we can easily create something similar using the expectations regex form:

```
cljapplied/src/ch8/expect.clj
(expect #"java.lang.String cannot be cast to java.lang.Number"
  (try (doall (range "boom"))
       (catch ClassCastException e (.getMessage e))))
```

Another area where the expectations library differs from clojure.test is in performing a deeper analysis when an assertion fails so that a more detailed explanation of the failure can be provided. This is particularly helpful for comparing complex nested collections.

---

1. https://github.com/jaycfields/expectations

For example, consider the following test, which mistakenly decrements an internal value inside a hash-map instead of incrementing it:

cljapplied/src/ch8/expect.clj
```
(expect {:a {:b 2}} (update-in {:a {:b 1}} [:a :b] dec))
```

When this test is run, the value for :b will be 0 instead of 2, which we can see in the following output:

```
failure in (expect.clj:20) : ch8.expect
(expect {:a {:b 2}} (update-in {:a {:b 1}} [:a :b] dec))

        expected: {:a {:b 2}}
            was: {:a {:b 0}}

        in expected, not actual: {:a {:b 2}}
        in actual, not expected: {:a {:b 0}}
```

The equivalent failure in clojure.test would have looked like this:

```
FAIL in (test-update-in) (NO_SOURCE_FILE:1)
expected: (= {:a {:b 2}} (update-in {:a {:b 1}} [:a :b] dec))
  actual: (not (= {:a {:b 2}} {:a {:b 0}}))
```

For data structures of this size, it's relatively easy to spot the differences, but this result diffing is helpful for examining larger pieces of data.

expectations has a number of additional features not addressed here. If your interest is piqued, it may be worth examining it further as an alternative to clojure.test. The preference in test definition is a matter of personal taste.

Developers coming from Java, Ruby, or many other popular languages will be familiar with this style of example-based testing, perhaps even finding it synonymous with unit testing. Another style of unit testing that's popular in the Clojure community is *property-based* testing (also known as *generative* testing).

Property-Based Tests with test.check

Example-based tests rely on developers to enumerate enough examples to fully verify the behavior of the functions under test. Each additional example covers one more input and verifies its output. Property-based tests instead encourage you to look for *properties* of your functions that are always true. You can then use *generators* to produce a large number of random examples that can be fed into your code. For each generated example you can verify that the property holds true.

Property-based tests generally involve more time invested in assembling data generators and thinking carefully about the properties of our code. However, once we've created the generators and properties, we can produce an arbitrary number of examples. Anecdotally, the time spent defining good properties also helps increase code clarity.

Consider the range function we've already looked at with clojure.test. When we invoke range with a single argument, we expect a range of numbers from 0 to that number, exclusive. We must then consider what properties we can check. For example, the count of the output sequence should equal the input value. Let's write this as a test.check property.

First we require a few useful namespaces from test.check:

cljapplied/src/ch8/check.clj
```
(:require [clojure.test.check :as tc]
          [clojure.test.check.generators :as gen]
          [clojure.test.check.properties :as prop])
```

Then range-count-eq-n defines a property that we expect to hold true in our code:

cljapplied/src/ch8/check.clj
```
(def range-count-eq-n
  (prop/for-all [n gen/int]
    (= n (count (range n)))))
```

The prop/for-all declares inputs bound to values from a generator and a body expression that should be true. In this case, we use gen/int to generate random integers.

We can then run quick-check to validate this property for 100 different random inputs:

```
user=> (use 'ch8.check)
user=> (in-ns 'ch8.check)
ch8.check=> (tc/quick-check 100 range-count-eq-n)
{:result false,
 :seed 1423719392783,
 :failing-size 2,
 :num-tests 3,
 :fail [-1],
 :shrunk {:total-nodes-visited 1, :depth 0, :result false, :smallest [-1]}}
```

This test fails because the property doesn't hold. The quick-check function ran three tests before finding an error with the input -1. We didn't think about what happens with a negative range index; in that case, we get the empty list instead. We need to fine-tune our generator to check this property for only nonnegative integers by replacing gen/int with gen/pos-int:

cljapplied/src/ch8/check.clj
```
(def range-count-eq-n-pos
  (prop/for-all [n gen/pos-int]
    (= n (count (range n)))))
```

```
ch8.check=> (tc/quick-check 100 range-count-eq-n-pos)
{:result true, :num-tests 100, :seed 1423720335630}
```

Now the test passes with 100 successful runs. We might also want to verify properties like the first element being equal to the starting value, the last value being less than end, and the step size between elements.

Instead let's look at applying test.check to something more interesting: the ingredient unit conversions we defined in Chapter 1, *Model Your Domain*, on page 3. To refresh your memory, here are the Ingredient record definition and conversion functions:

cljapplied/src/ch1/validate.clj
```
(defrecord Ingredient
  [name     ;; string
   quantity ;; amount
   unit     ;; keyword
   ])
```

cljapplied/src/ch1/convert.clj
```
(defmulti convert
  "Convert quantity from unit1 to unit2, matching on [unit1 unit2]"
  (fn [unit1 unit2 quantity] [unit1 unit2]))

;; lb to oz
(defmethod convert [:lb :oz] [_ _ lb] (* lb 16))

;; oz to lb
(defmethod convert [:oz :lb] [_ _ oz] (/ oz 16))

;; fallthrough
(defmethod convert :default [u1 u2 q]
  (if (= u1 u2)
    q
    (assert false (str "Unknown unit conversion from " u1 " to " u2))))

(defn ingredient+
  "Add two ingredients into a single ingredient, combining their
  quantities with unit conversion if necessary."
  [{q1 :quantity u1 :unit :as i1} {q2 :quantity u2 :unit}]
  (assoc i1 :quantity (+ q1 (convert u2 u1 q2))))
```

The first function, convert, converts a quantity in one unit to another. It's defined as a multimethod to allow open extension later on as we add more units. The ingredient+ function is used to add two of the same ingredient together, including any unit conversion. And finally, the shopping-list function takes a recipe and builds a shopping list, combining ingredients if necessary.

To test these functions using property-based testing, we'll need to define generators to produce random inputs (ingredients, recipes, and so on) and some properties that should hold true when these functions are invoked. Let's start by building up our data generators.

Generating Ingredients and Recipes

The test.check library contains a namespace full of existing generators for most of the primitive types in Clojure, collections of primitives, tuples, maps, and other helpful combinators. For our purposes we know, looking at our function inputs, that we need to create random ingredients and recipes.

We'll start with generating random ingredients. We need to first consider how to generate random valid values for each of the properties of an ingredient. For names, we can either generate random strings using a provided generator like gen/string-alpha-numeric or define a set of valid ingredient names. Because it'll be useful later to match ingredients based on name, we'll use the latter strategy:

cljapplied/src/ch8/check.clj
```
(def gen-food
  (gen/elements ["flour" "sugar" "butter"]))
```

The gen/elements function returns a generator that will randomly choose elements from the provided collection, which we tested earlier with gen/sample.

Similarly, we'll use gen/elements to produce random units of measure:

cljapplied/src/ch8/check.clj
```
(def gen-unit
  (gen/elements [:oz :lb]))
```

Now we have enough generators to produce full random ingredient entities. We have no generator for records, but we can produce random record instances either by using gen/tuple to create inputs for ->Ingredient or gen/hash-map for map->Ingredient. We'll take the latter approach:

cljapplied/src/ch8/check.clj
```
(def gen-ingredient
  (gen/fmap map->Ingredient
    (gen/hash-map
      :name gen-food
      :quantity gen/s-pos-int
      :unit gen-unit)))
```

In this example gen/hash-map is used to generate hash-maps with a known set of keys and generators for the values. This is the data we'll use to create each random ingredient. We then use gen/fmap to create a new generator by applying a function to the values returned from the first generator. Here we apply the map->Ingredient factory function to the generated values of gen/hash-map.

Testing this generator with gen/sample, we can see a few test examples:

```
#check.recipe.Ingredient{:name "sugar", :quantity 1, :unit :oz}
#check.recipe.Ingredient{:name "sugar", :quantity 1, :unit :lb}
#check.recipe.Ingredient{:name "butter", :quantity 3, :unit :lb}
#check.recipe.Ingredient{:name "flour", :quantity 3, :unit :oz}
#check.recipe.Ingredient{:name "flour", :quantity 5, :unit :lb}
#check.recipe.Ingredient{:name "sugar", :quantity 6, :unit :lb}
```

Now that we have generators for units, food, and ingredients, we can define some properties for our functions.

Testing with Properties

When describing the properties of our code, we're looking for *invariants*— properties that are always true. Some common kinds of invariants are mathematical laws, relationships between inputs and outputs, round-trip or complementing functions, and comparing action effects.

Mathematical properties such as identity, associativity, commutativity, and idempotency are an excellent place to start. Let's consider how an identity property might apply to the convert function. If you convert a quantity of one unit to the same unit, you expect the same value back. Here's how we can encode this as a property:

cljapplied/src/ch8/check.clj
```
(def identity-conversion-prop
  (prop/for-all [u gen-unit
                 n gen/s-pos-int]
    (= n (convert u u n))))
```

The identity-conversion-prop is a test-check property that says for all units u and positive integers n, converting to the same u must return n.

We can run quick-check to verify that this property holds:

cljapplied/src/ch8/check.clj
```
(def conversion-order-prop
  (prop/for-all [u1 gen-unit
                 u2 gen-unit
                 u3 gen-unit
                 u4 gen-unit
                 n gen/s-pos-int]
```

```
     (= (->> n (convert u1 u2) (convert u2 u3) (convert u3 u4))
        (->> n (convert u1 u3) (convert u3 u2) (convert u2 u4)))))
```

```
=> (tc/quick-check 100 identity-conversion-prop)
{:result true, :num-tests 100, :seed 1424055070008}
```

Looking beyond identity, we can see that conversion through two different intermediate units should yield the same answer if the conversions are applied in either order. We can encode this in a property:

cljapplied/src/ch8/check.clj
```
(def conversion-order-prop
  (prop/for-all [u1 gen-unit
                 u2 gen-unit
                 u3 gen-unit
                 u4 gen-unit
                 n gen/s-pos-int]
    (= (->> n (convert u1 u2) (convert u2 u3) (convert u3 u4))
       (->> n (convert u1 u3) (convert u3 u2) (convert u2 u4)))))
```

Another common kind of invariant concerns complementary or round-trip operations. These could be encode and decode, serialize and deserialize, put and get, or create and delete. In general, all of these pairs of operations should yield a result equal to the starting value. For conversion, we want to test that conversion in either direction yields the starting value:

cljapplied/src/ch8/check.clj
```
(def roundtrip-conversion-prop
  (prop/for-all [u1 gen-unit u2 gen-unit
                 q gen/s-pos-int]
    (and (= q
            (convert u1 u2 (convert u2 u1 q))
            (convert u2 u1 (convert u1 u2 q))))))
```

This is a good start for testing properties of the convert function. Let's take a look at ingredient+ and think about invariants for adding together ingredients of different units. Consider the associative property for adding ingredients:

cljapplied/src/ch8/check.clj
```
(defn add-and-convert [i1 i2 i3 output-unit]
  (let [{:keys [quantity unit]} (ingredient+ i1 (ingredient+ i2 i3))]
    (convert unit output-unit quantity)))

(def associative-ingredient+-prop
  (prop/for-all [i1 gen-ingredient
                 i2 gen-ingredient
                 i3 gen-ingredient]
    (= (add-and-convert i1 i2 i3 (:unit i1))
       (add-and-convert i3 i1 i2 (:unit i1))
       (add-and-convert i2 i1 i3 (:unit i1)))))
```

We define a helper function that adds three ingredients, then converts to a specified output unit. This allows us to compare several orderings against a common output unit in associative-ingredient+-prop.

We've been defining all of these properties by themselves and checking them with quick-check, but we can also integrate them into a standard clojure.test build by replacing def with clojure.test.check.clojure-test/defspec in each of the preceding properties.

When you apply these techniques to your own code, you'll find that creating generators and defining properties will force you to consider your code from a new perspective. Generators cause you to reexamine exactly what set of inputs you expect to receive in your functions. Often when creating composite generators you'll discover inputs that violate your assumptions, forcing you to make your functions more robust.

Similarly, defining properties requires clarifying the invariants in your code. Invariants are important because they reduce the number of cases your code must consider, making the code simpler and clearer. On the flip side, they also allow your code to fail early if an invariant has been violated.

Wrapping Up

No one technique detects every problem. Strategic investments in a variety of testing techniques are the best way to get a great return on your testing effort. REPL-based testing helps us develop in small increments, making sure that each expression does what we expect. Example-based testing allows us to capture any interesting examples we discover during REPL testing, ensuring that special cases are covered by any future changes. Property-based testing clarifies our thinking and provides coverage from a wide variety of inputs. These techniques work together to give us validation that our code does what we expect.

## CHAPTER 9

Formatting Data

So far we've concerned ourselves mostly with data and code that lives inside our application. Modern software, however, usually requires communication with file systems, other processes, and remote software. Web servers talk with browsers, applications send messages to queueing systems, and scripts build entire stacks with descriptions—all communicating with others in various ways.

In the next few pages, we'll explore some of Clojure's facilities for communicating with other programs and resources, and the tools and techniques that facilitate this. The data we're concerned with in this chapter is *serializable* data.

Data Serialization Formats

Serializable data is data that can be stored, translated into other formats, and therefore exchanged with other programs. Well-defined serialization formats facilitate this exchange.

Here's a likely scenario: you have a source process sending data to a target process. The two processes have each been written a different language and run within distinct operating systems on varying processor architectures. Naturally, the bits containing the data within the source process differ from the bits the target process would use to represent the data. The source process needs to serialize its data into a common format that the target process can understand. The target process will deserialize the common format into a native representation.

This is simple enough in concept. In practice, the decision about which data serialization format to use can often be confounding. Questions that arise may include:

- Will the data and format ever need to be read by people?
- Will the data require a schema for validation?
- Will the *format* require validation?
- Will the schema change over time, and require versions?
- Will the data need to conform to a standard?

Practical concerns also arise:

- Are libraries available to help in your language of choice?
- Will serialization and deserialization be fast enough?
- How much is the structure of the data likely to change over time?
- How much control do you require over how the data is consumed?

These (and other) questions have led to many, many serialization formats being created over time.

Let's look at a few of the more widely used data formats in the Clojure space: specifically, the Extensible Data Notation (edn) and JavaScript Object Notation (JSON) text formats; and Transit, which can serialize into either text or binary formats.

Let's start as close to home as possible, with edn.

Extensible Data Notation

The edn format is a text-serialization format often used with Clojure. Programs written in the Clojure language are represented in a superset of the edn format. Given its close wiring into the language, edn is an easy choice for reading and writing data. Although edn is most commonly seen in the Clojure community, implementations are available in other languages.[1]

Representing a product catalog in edn would take the following form:

```
[{:num    112
  :dept   :clothing
  :desc   "V-Neck T-Shirt"
  :item-attributes {
    :sizing {:type :general :size :large}
    :color :blue
    :manufacturer-id 11250
    :categories #{:mens :shirts :undershirts :vneck :premium}}
  :price #pricing/money "$55.35"}
 {:num    113
  :dept   :clothing
  :desc   "Flat-Front Slacks"
  :item-attributes {
```

---

1.   https://github.com/edn-format/edn/wiki/Implementations

```
    :size  {:type :measured :waist 32 :length 36 }
    :color :charcoal
    :manufacturer-id 17234
    :categories #{:mens :pants :dress-pants :premium}}
  :price #pricing/money "$79.99"}
 ,,,
]
```

All of the built-in data types you're used to in Clojure are perfectly acceptable in edn, and extensions are possible (for example, #pricing/money). Unsurprisingly, a vector of nested maps contains the data. The serialization format looks no different than if it were present in your program code.

Let's look at how to get edn data into and out of our system.

Reading edn

The clojure.edn namespace provides functions for reading edn into Clojure, along with a few neat additional features.[2] You can read edn in from a string with the clojure.edn/read-string function.

Suppose the following collection of users is stored in users.edn:

```
[
  {:name  "Joe Smith"
   :email "joe@company.com"
   :roles [:admin :supervisor :analyst]}
  {:name  "Robert Jones"
   :email "rob@company.com"
   :roles [:analyst]}
]
```

You can read this data from the users.edn file to initialize a login system or contact list, as part of your initial system configuration:

```
(require '[clojure.edn :as edn])

(def users (atom []))

(defn init-users []
  (reset! users
    (edn/read-string (slurp "users.edn"))))
```

During your application's initialization process, a call to init-users will reset the value of users to its initial value.

edn files serve well as application configuration, and you'll often see .edn files used in this capacity.

---

2. https://github.com/edn-format/edn

The clojure.edn/read-string function will read the first form found in the data string; if you want more-complex data, you'll need either multiple strings (or streams), a data structure containing the desired data, or multiple calls to read.

We recommend always using the clojure.edn namespace when reading in edn data. It's tempting to avoid using clojure.edn and use Clojure's read functions to get data into the system more directly—the function in Clojure is also read-string—but by default Clojure's read functions (such as read-string) read *and* execute any Clojure source passed to them:

```
user=> (read-string "#=(println \"WHAT?!\")")
WHAT?!
nil
```

This kind of behavior can be dangerous, allowing arbitrary code execution. You may want to be on the lookout for read-string in libraries you're including, or in code you've written previously.

In Clojure 1.5 and higher, you can reliably avoid dangerous behavior by binding *read-eval* to false. Binding *read-eval* sets the safety on and avoids arbitrary code execution. If for whatever reason you *must* use Clojure's read-string without the safety on, you should only read from trusted sources.

edn Values

The edn specification contains a list of value types that languages implementing the spec must be able to handle. These values types should look familiar to a Clojurist:

- nil—nil represents a nil, null, or nothing value.

- Boolean—true and false correspond to Clojure's true and false values.

- Characters: When \ is followed by character, the character value is used. For instance, \c represents the letter c. When followed by a u and four hex digits, a Unicode value is represented (\u03BB is the λ character). A few special characters, such as \newline and \tab, are also available.

- Strings—Strings are double-quoted, as in "this is a string".

- Numbers—Integers (1234) and floating-point numbers (1.234) are both supported, and they can be prefixed with a - to indicate a negative number.

- Symbols—edn symbols follow the rules for Clojure symbols. Symbols can use namespace-like notation (my-namespace/symbol-name).

- Keywords—The same rules as for symbols are used, with a : prepended. Unlike in Clojure, :: can't be used to indicate a namespace-qualified keyword, since edn data does not define namespaces.

- Collections—edn allows lists (), sets #{}, maps {}, and vectors []. The rules are identical to Clojure's.

edn has two extended primitives: #inst and #uuid. An #inst represents a fixed point in time: #inst "1982-01-16T23:20:50.52Z" is January 16, 1982 at 11:20:50.52 UTC. A #uuid is a 128-bit unique identifier.[3]

In addition to having the built-in value types and extensions, edn delivers on its promise of extensibility via support for *tagged literals*.

Extending edn with Tagged Literals

Obviously, not every type of data you want to serialize is represented in the preceding list. Clojure provides a mechanism for extensibility through edn, in the form of tagged literals. Tagged literals allow you to create your own custom primitives, as portable representations of custom classes.

When present in edn data, the tag is not explicitly bound to a reader function or any particular representation type. Every program can interpret the same tag using different reader functions.

Tagged literals have the following form:

```
#namespace/symbol data
```

Representing a custom primitive using a tagged literal has a few steps. First, define the representation of the value in the program. Next, create a reader that can create an instance of the representation. Finally, you must tell Clojure how to recognize the new tag, sending its reader macro to the dispatch table. (Optionally, you can also create a printer that renders the tag when using print.)

Let's represent a custom primitive—a playing card—using a tagged literal definition. We'll use a string to represent the rank and suit of the playing card: 2h will represent the two of hearts, for example. Ranks are the numbers 2 through 9; the letters T, J, Q, K, and A are ten, jack, queen, king, and ace, respectively. The suits are the lowercase letters c, d, h, and s.

The complete tag should look like #my/card "2h".

---

3.   http://en.wikipedia.org/wiki/Universally_unique_identifier

Given this specification, we'll need to represent the card in our program. We'll use a record with characters representing the rank and suit:

cards/src/cards/cards.clj
```
(defrecord Card [rank suit])
```

We could create a record using the usual constructor, but we'd like to ensure that the card is a valid representation. Additionally, we'd like to represent (and read) a card as a two-character string. To do that, we'll create a reader that can read our two-character string representation, validate the input, and produce the proper record instance:

cards/src/cards/cards.clj
```
(def ranks "23456789TJQKA")
(def suits "hdcs")

(defn- check [val vals]
  (if (some #{val} (set vals))
    val
    (throw (IllegalArgumentException.
             (format "Invalid value: %s, expected: %s" val vals)))))

(defn card-reader [card]
  (let [[rank suit] card]
    (->Card (check rank ranks) (check suit suits))))
```

The card-reader reads a card's string representation and splits the string into rank and suit characters. It then validates that both the rank and the suit come from the expected character sets and constructs an instance of the Card.

Let's try out the reader by itself:

```
user> (card-reader "2c")
#user.Card{:rank \2, :suit \c}
```

The most common way that a library or application provides Clojure with reader mappings is via a data_readers.clj file in the classpath. (As of Clojure 1.7, data_readers.cljc is also supported.) Clojure loads all such files at startup. This file is expected to contain a literal Clojure map structure in which the keys are symbols (the tags) and the values are symbols referring to the reader function vars.

In the context of a library, including a data_readers file can create situations in which the application using the library develops unexpected behavior. Instead, you can choose to provide the associated reader functions and an example of how to configure the reader map in the application. The application's author can then choose what to include and exclude.

Based on this info, Clojure knows when it sees the tag #my/card to read the data and invoke cards/card-reader:

```
{my/card cards/card-reader}
```

Notice that the namespace of the tag doesn't need to match the namespace of the reader or record.

It's also possible to dynamically supply tagged literal readers in the code by binding the *data-readers* var around the read:

```
(binding [*data-readers* {'my/card #'cards/card-reader}]
  (read-string "#my/card \"2c\""))
```

Finally, it's possible we'll eventually want to *write*, not just read, our cards, so we need to build a print writer. To do this, we take advantage of the print-dup multimethod to output the format we're expecting to read back in later:

```
cards/src/cards/cards.clj
(defn card-str [card]
  (str "#my/card \"" (:rank card) (:suit card) "\""))

(defmethod print-method cards.Card [card ^java.io.Writer w]
  (.write w (card-str card)))

(defmethod print-dup cards.Card [card w]
  (print-method card w))
```

One final trick we can play is to provide a custom function that handles unknown tags. By default the reader will throw a RuntimeException if it encounters an unknown tag, but we can provide our own function by binding *default-data-reader-fn*. This hook allows us to dynamically understand and react to tags, perhaps by mapping them to a dynamic set of reader tags.

A Shortcut

If creating a tagged literal seems like quite a bit of work, you can consider using Steve Miner's tagged library,[4] which automates tag creation for records.

Writing Text Formats to a File

edn is a text-serializable format: all the work we've done so far yields a string. This string can be written to a file like any other, using Clojure's writer facility:

```
(defn write-text-to-file [text f]
  (with-open [w (clojure.java.io/writer f)]
    (.write w text))))
```

---

4. https://github.com/miner/tagged

If you've created any tagged literals, you'll need to create a printer for them so that they serialize correctly.

Any text-serializable format creates a string and can be written using the same pattern. This applies equally to our next format: JSON.

JSON

JSON[5] has become one of the more common data formats for dealing with web applications and data exchange. It's human-readable, and many resources are available for its use. These two factors make it an attractive option as a data format.

The fundamental concepts in JSON are the *object* and the *array*, as the two container types for any values in the data. Objects correspond strongly to Clojure's hash-maps, being an set of key-value pairs. Arrays are ordered lists of arbitrary data and most closely resemble a vector in Clojure.

If we convert the users.edn file from earlier to users.json, it looks like this:

```
[
  {"name":   "Joe Smith"
   "email": "joe@company.com"
   "roles": ["admin", "supervisor", "analyst"]},
  {"name":   "Robert Jones"
   "email": "rob@company.com"
   "roles": ["analyst"]}
]
```

JSON Values

JSON's list of built-in values is somewhat more limited than edn's, but for most developers it's enough to work with:

- null—null represents a nil, null, or nothing value.

- Boolean—true and false correspond to JavaScript's true and false values.

- Strings—Strings are double-quoted, as in "this is a string".

- Numbers—Integers (1234) and floating-point numbers (1.234) are both supported, and they can be prefixed with a - to indicate a negative number.

- Arrays—Arrays are enclosed in brackets [] and contain comma-separated values. Arrays can contain values of varying types, and array values remain ordered.

---

5.   http://json.org

- Objects—Objects are wrapped in braces {}. An object is a collection of comma-separated key-value pairs. The order of key-value pairs in an object isn't guaranteed, similar to Clojure's map.

JSON's number handling gets something of a bad rap. The JSON spec places integers at 64 bits, whereas current browser implementations of JavaScript limit the length of integers to 2^{53}.

JSON and Clojure

Clojure provides an idiomatic JSON parsing library—data.json[6]—for handling JSON in Clojure. It's straightforward to use, providing read-str and write-str functions that do exactly what you might expect:

```
user=> (require '[clojure.data.json :as j])
user=> (j/read-str "[{\"name\": \"Ben\", \"age\": 39},
                      {\"name\": \"Monster\", \"age\": 4}]")
[{"name" "Ben", "age" 39} {"name" "Monster", "age" 4}]

user=> (j/write-str [{:name "Christina"}, {:name "Mina" :age 3}])
"[{\"name\":\"Christina\"},{\"age\":3,\"name\":\"Mina\"}]"
```

Clojure's data.json library, however, lags behind in terms of features, speed, and symmetric reading and writing. Instead, let's have a look at Lee Hinman's Cheshire[7] library, powered by the Jackson Project's JSON parser for Java.[8]

Reading and writing in Cheshire are simple enough, using generate-string and parse-string, respectively:

```
user=> (require '[cheshire.core :refer :all])
user=> (parse-string "[{\"name\": \"Ben\", \"age\": 39},
                        {\"name\": \"Monster\", \"age\": 4}]")
({"name" "Ben", "age" 39} {"name" "Monster", "age" 4})

user=> (generate-string [{:name "Christina"}, {:name "Mina" :age 3}])
"[{\"name\":\"Christina\"},{\"name\":\"Mina\",\"age\":3}]"
```

With Cheshire, if your data contains keywords as map keys, those are represented as strings (as in data.json). When parsing back in, parse-string takes a second parameter to indicate that string keys should be converted to keywords:

```
user=> (parse-string "[{\"name\": \"Ben\", \"age\": 39},
                        {\"name\": \"Monster\", \"age\": 4}]" true)
({:name "Ben", :age 39} {:name "Monster", :age 4})
```

---

6. https://github.com/clojure/data.json
7. https://github.com/dakrone/cheshire
8. https://github.com/FasterXML/jackson

Cheshire supports encoding additional data types via the add-encoder function in the cheshire.generate namespace. JSON doesn't include a format for dates, and the default date encoding is less than satisfactory:

```
user=> (generate-string {:date (java.util.Date.)})
"{\"date\":\"2015-05-15T03:30:43Z\"}"
```

Note that the date doesn't include time-offset information or fractional seconds. If we want to encode the date in full ISO 8601 format, we need to write a custom encoder. This requires a little setup to format the date, using a Simple-DateFormat *and* a string format for the date:

```
cljapplied/src/ch9/date_fmt.clj
(def ^:private date-format
  (proxy [ThreadLocal] []
    (initialValue []
      (doto (java.text.SimpleDateFormat. "yyyy-MM-dd'T'HH:mm:ss.SSSXXX")))))))

(defn- format-inst
  "Create a tolerable string from an inst"
  [d]
  (str "#inst (.format (.get date-format) d)"))

(defn- date-part
  "Extract the date part of a stringified #inst"
  [d]
  (second (re-matches #"#inst (.*)" d)))
```

We can then use these functions to add an encoder to Cheshire when we're encoding our date:

```
user=> (add-encoder java.util.Date
  #_=>    (fn [d generator]
  #_=>      (.writeString generator (format-inst d))))
nil

user=> (generate-string {:date (java.util.Date.)})
"{\"date\":\"#inst 2015-05-14T23:57:23.554-04:00\"}"
```

The problem with this custom encoding—and any custom encoding—is that to decode it, we must write a corresponding custom decoder. Cheshire doesn't support inline custom decoders at present.

The data.json library *does* support both custom encoding and decoding, at the cost of speed. By passing a :key-fn and :value-fn, we can resolve most problems. We need to create read and write functions that handle the date tolerably to pass as the :value-fn. In both cases, we're checking the key for a :date keyword, and if we find it, applying a function to either read or write the date according to our expectations:

cljapplied/src/ch9/date_fmt.clj
```
(defn read-date [k v]
  (if (= :date k)
      (.parse (.get date-format) (date-part v))
      v))

(defn write-date [k v]
  (if (= :date k)
      (str "#inst " (.format (.get date-format) v))
      v))
```

We can now use these functions (via the ch9.date-fmt namespace) when writing and reading to correctly serialize the date:

```
user=> (require '[ch9.date-fmt :as df])
user=> (require '[clojure.data.json :as j])

user=> (j/write-str {:keyword "string",
  #_=>                :date (java.util.Date.)}
  #_=>                :value-fn df/write-date)
"{\"keyword\":\"string\",\"date\":\"#inst 2015-05-10T15:15:31.626-04:00\"}"

user=> (j/read-str
  #_=>    (j/write-str {:keyword "string",
  #_=>                 :date (java.util.Date.)}
  #_=>                 :value-fn df/write-date)
  #_=>    :key-fn keyword
  #_=>    :value-fn df/read-date)
{:keyword "string", :date #inst "2015-05-10T19:15:36.314-00:00"}
```

This should feel fairly familiar after learning about the reader and writer necessary for an implementation of a tagged literal. You'll often find yourself writing a custom serializer for oddities in your data, and even sometimes for common elements.

Serialization Trade-offs

It's easy to see that as the number of extended serializable types grows, this approach could get unwieldy. And we're still left with a more fundamental problem: whatever encoding you choose when serializing a particular type of data, there must be a corresponding decoder for that type of data that's understood by consumers.

JSON remains a popular choice for serialization, especially when serving data directly to browsers and JavaScript applications. Many developer-hours have been spent making JavaScript's native JSON parser fast and efficient. The Jackson JSON parser for Java is also reasonably snappy. Even so, JSON is still a text-serialization format. As such, neither the Jackson parser or Java-

Script's native parser can hold a candle to the speed and efficiency of binary serialization formats such as Fressian[9] and MessagePack.[10]

The high performance of binary serialization formats stems from several factors. Binary data doesn't require the same degree of work to convert from strings to native representation for primitive types. Binary encodings can both be compressed and make use of internal caching in ways that text encodings can't without losing human readability. Even without compression and caching, binary representations can be much smaller.

For instance, a phone number in the United States can be represented as three integers: area code, prefix, and line number. These could be represented in binary as three short integers, totaling 48 bits. The same number represented as a Unicode string is 160 bits. In a list of a million phone numbers, the difference between these accounts for over 13MB of data.

The trade-off tends to be development time. Despite its superior performance, writing a Fressian library to handle application-specific types requires a fair amount of effort. The same extensions for edn data would be much easier. However, selling edn against other data formats with greater mindshare and more-mature tooling in other language communities is an uphill battle.

JSON falls somewhere between the two: it has strong tooling and wide mindshare. If a binary format is needed, it's available via the SMILE format,[11] a JSON-compatible, self-describing binary format. Many developers are comfortable enough with JSON that they can use it to string-encode the things they need.

If we pull back a level, an attractive hybrid option is available: Transit. Transit has a readable verbose format for humans but can also use either a compact JSON format with caching capabilities or a binary format using MessagePack. It has a simple extension mechanism. It takes advantage of existing high-performance parsers in JavaScript and Java.

Let's dig in and get our heads around Transit.

Transit

Transit[12] is a relative newcomer to the world of data interchange, thoughtfully developed to solve a problem many have wrestled with: how to communicate

---

9.   https://github.com/Datomic/fressian
10. http://msgpack.org/
11. http://wiki.fasterxml.com/SmileFormat
12. http://transit-format.org

extensible typed values cleanly and quickly regardless of language. With its release came several implementations (Clojure, ClojureScript, Java, JavaScript, Ruby, and Python), and more have been developed subsequently.

Fundamentally, Transit is an extensible metaformat that sits atop either JSON or MessagePack, and a collection of client libraries that handle the translation of Transit-encoded typed values into language-native values. We'll be using transit-clj,[13] since we're working in Clojure.

Transit data has a verbose form that's somewhat human-readable and compact forms that encode and cache repeated data. To create this data, you need to create a writer using the provided cognitect.transit/writer function. This takes an output stream as a write target, and an encoding, along with an optional map of options. You can then use the write function from the resulting writer to write to the output stream:

```
(require '[cognitect.transit :as transit])
(import [java.io ByteArrayInputStream ByteArrayOutputStream])

(def output (ByteArrayOutputStream. 4096))
(def writer (transit/writer output :json-verbose))

(transit/write writer [
  {:name  "Joe Smith"
   :email "joe@company.com"
   :roles [:admin :supervisor :analyst]}
  {:name  "Robert Jones"
   :email "rob@company.com"
   :roles [:analyst]}
])
```

At this point, output contains the bytes that Transit has written in :json-verbose format. If we were to have a look inside of output, we'd see that the encoding Transit has done looks almost but not quite entirely like JSON:

```
[{"~:email": "joe@company.com",
  "~:name":  "Joe Smith",
  "~:roles": ["~:admin","~:supervisor","~:analyst"]},

{"~:email": "rob@company.com",
  "~:name":  "Robert Jones",
  "~:roles": ["~:analyst"]}]
```

If we run the process again using :json in place of :json-verbose, the results are more cryptic:

---

13. https://github.com/cognitect/transit-clj

```
[
 ["^ ","~:email", "joe@company.com",
     "~:name",  "Joe Smith",
     "~:roles", ["~:admin","~:supervisor","~:analyst"]],
 ["^ ","^0",     "rob@company.com",
     "^1",       "Robert Jones",
     "^2",       ["^5"]]
]
```

We've added spacing to make the differences more obvious. In the second data set, some of the keys and data have been replaced with ^n. When Transit encounters certain data types (in this case, keywords), it caches the value. When that data is reused, it simply puts the cache marker in its place. For example, ^5 is replaced with ~:analyst when Transit reads this value back.

The ~ character prefacing the keywords is an indicator that the thing that follows is an instance of one of Transit's extension types, as opposed to a ground type. As it happens, ~: indicates that the value is a keyword. Transit provides both extensibility through implementation of read- and write-handlers, and performance via its encoding and caching techniques. For these reasons, it's a strong candidate for a serialization format in any application.

Transit Values

Given that the authors of Transit are also the authors of Clojure, you might expect that the value types would be similar, and you wouldn't be disappointed. Transit supports ground types and extension types, some of which correspond to underlying Java types. The ground types are:

- null—null represents nil, null, or nothing values (yes, still).
- Strings—Strings are double-quoted, and are java.lang.Strings.
- Booleans—true and false correspond to Clojure's true and false (implemented as java.lang.Boolean).
- Integers—Integer types are coerced into a java.lang.Long.
- Decimals—Like integers, floats and doubles are coerced into java.lang.Double.

The extension types (when deserialized into Clojure data) are:

- Keywords—A keyword represents a clojure.lang.Keyword.
- Symbols—A symbol represents a clojure.lang.Symbol.
- Big decimal—This is represented internally as a java.math.BigDecimal.
- Big integer—This is represented as clojure.lang.BigInt.
- Time—An instant in time is stored as a java.util.Date.
- URI—URIs are represented as com.cognitect.Transit.URI.

- Link: A link, from the Collection+JSON media type, is stored as a cognitect.Transit.Link.
- UUID—An identifier represents a java.util.UUID.
- char—This is a single character, using java.lang.Character.
- Collections—Transit accepts lists, sets, maps, and vectors. These all behave as expected, and are emitted as the appropriate Clojure type.
- Ratios—Ratios are an included tagged extension type, stored as clojure.lang.Ratio.

Unlike the rest of the included types, a Ratio has no representation in the Transit included types. It's a custom tagged extension included with the transit-clj library. There's nothing fundamentally special about a Ratio. Transit provides an extension mechanism you can use to encode your own custom data shapes.

Transit in Clojure

Because Transit packs the Clojure native types effectively, it's a good fit for exchanging data with other processes—provided they have a Transit client. The availability of clients is the primary limiter of Transit.

One of the features that makes Transit attractive is the ability to extend its types set via tagged extensions. Adding an extension is no more difficult than it is in edn, so let's give it a try.

When (not if) you build an invoice payment system, you'll need to represent money in something other than a decimal. In *Constructing Entities*, on page 6 we introduced Money and Currency records, which we'll use as the basis for our payment system. Let's review the setup:

cljapplied/src/ch1/money.clj
```
(ns ch1.money)

(declare validate-same-currency)

(defrecord Currency [divisor sym desc])

(defrecord Money [amount ^Currency currency]
  java.lang.Comparable
    (compareTo [m1 m2]
      (validate-same-currency m1 m2)
      (compare (:amount m1) (:amount m2))))

(def currencies {:usd (->Currency 100 "USD" "US Dollars")
                 :eur (->Currency 100 "EUR" "Euro")})
```

The sym field is an abbreviation by which the currency can be identified (for example, USD or EUR). The divisor is the number that the amount part of a Money value should be divided by to get the integral unit value. For US dollars, 100 cents equals one dollar, so the divisor would be 100.

In Money, the amount field represents the smallest unit of currency (cents in USD). The currency field is a Currency record. This could also be implemented as a keyword that identifies the currency, but we're choosing to embed the value directly. We are, however, including a map of keywords to predefined Currency values for convenience.

To use these values in Transit (specifically, transit-clj), we need to add read and write handlers for each. These maps will be passed to the writer when the writer is created. The write handlers are defined like this:

cljapplied/src/ch9/money_transit.clj
```
(def write-handlers {
  Currency
  (reify WriteHandler
    (tag [_ _] "currency")
    (rep [_ c] [(:divisor c) (:sym c) (:desc c)])
    (stringRep [_ _] nil)
    (getVerboseHandler [_] nil))

  Money
  (reify WriteHandler
    (tag [_ m] "money")
    (rep [_ m] [(:amount m) (:currency m)])
    (stringRep [_ _] nil)
    (getVerboseHandler [_] nil))})
```

In addition to the write handlers, we need to create corresponding read handlers:

cljapplied/src/ch9/money_transit.clj
```
(def read-handlers {
  "currency"
    (reify ReadHandler
      (fromRep [_ c] (apply ->Currency c)))
  "money"
    (reify ReadHandler
      (fromRep [_ m] (apply ->Money m)))})
```

With those pieces in place, we're ready to use the Transit client to read and write our data. We need to specify our read- and write-handlers as options to transit/writer and transit/reader, but otherwise the process is the same as before:

```
user=> (require '[ch1.money :refer :all]
  #_=>          '[ch9.money-transit :refer :all]
```

```
  #_=>             '[cognitect.transit :as transit])
user=> (import '[java.io ByteArrayInputStream ByteArrayOutputStream])

user=> (def output (ByteArrayOutputStream. 4096))
user=> (def writer (transit/writer output :json {:handlers write-handlers}))
user=> (def usd (->Currency 100 :usd))
user=> (def cash-out [(->Money 9900 usd)
  #_=>                (->Money 8500 usd)])
#'user/cash-out
user=> (transit/write writer cash-out)
nil
```

After we run through this, output contains a JSON-serialized, Transit-formatted
version of our data. If we were to look at it we'd see our data encoded exactly
as we specified:

```
[["~#money",[9900, ["~#currency",[100,"USD","US Dollars"]]]],
 ["^0",      [8500, ["^1",          [100,"USD","US Dollars"]]]]]
```

To read output back in, we create an input stream from output, create a reader,
and read in our newly minted data:

```
user=> (def input (ByteArrayInputStream. (.toByteArray output)))
#'user/input
user=> (def reader (transit/reader input :json {:handlers read-handlers}))
#'user/reader
user=> (def cash-in(transit/read reader))
#'user/cash-in
user=> cash-in
[#money.Money{:amount 9900,
              :currency #money.Currency{:divisor 100,
                                        :sym "USD",
                                        :desc "US Dollars"}}
 #money.Money{:amount 8500,
              :currency #money.Currency{:divisor 100,
                                        :sym "USD",
                                        :desc "US Dollars"}}]
user=> (= cash-in cash-out)
true
```

Perfect. The values we read are identical to the values we wrote, and available
in the application-specific record types. Nested custom types were handled
painlessly, and the types are portable.

As a data serialization format, Transit has a lot to recommend it. It *is* a newer
format, but with a feature set that'll enable quite a bit of growth. When adding
the ease with which it can be extended, it has the potential to become quite
popular. If you're not using Transit, you should bear it in mind for future
development.

Wrapping Up

Data serialization is serious business—a prerequisite for being able to exchange information with other processes. Many factors must be considered, not the least of which is the format you'll choose when sharing your data.

We've covered three of the most important formats for Clojure developers, enough to give you a taste of the joy and difficulty of shipping data outside of your process. Any one of the formats we've presented will get you started. This shouldn't be the end of your journey, however: data serialization is a complex landscape.

edn is near to Clojure in form, readable, and close to the hearts of Clojure developers. It isn't incredibly fast but works effectively for configuration. Its barrier to entry is low, and it can be extended via well-defined mechanisms.

JSON enjoys a broad footprint, especially for connecting to web browsers and JavaScript applications. This is primarily because of the many hours spent making it fast and its low barrier to entry. It's not as extensible as edn, and it's a little more fiddly to work with, but JSON can speak with a broader range of languages via its rich tooling.

Finally, Transit finds a good balance between extensibility and efficiency. Using existing parsers and formats as a transport mechanism, it delivers a quality development experience without sacrificing performance.

In the next chapter, you'll find several options for sharing your code and applications, not just your data.

## CHAPTER 10

Getting out the Door

At some point, either our pride as software developers compels us to publish things so our peers can see how clever we are, or our sense of altruism demands that we contribute something useful to make other people's lives easier. Let's take a minute to go beyond a public Git repo and consider the wider responsibilities of publication.

If you've never published a Clojure library or deployed a Clojure application into production, you likely have a number of questions. This chapter provides you with advice about publishing source code and libraries, as well as the deployment of Clojure applications into production environments. We'll look at decisions and trade-offs, including the duties of a responsible developer.

Software designs, system architectures, and deployment possibilities are widely diverse. When you're designing systems of significant size, you'll be considering a wide variety of options. A complete discussion of deployment and operational concerns is far beyond the scope of this book. Our intention here is to help you get a strong running start. Let's start with publishing source code.

Publish Your Code

If you have a tidbit of code that other developers may find useful or demonstrative, or a library that solves a common problem, you can release the source code to the public. In this section, we'll talk about the decisions involved in both.

Contributing code to the public has some consequences, not the least of which is that you'll be expected to maintain and respond to questions about your project, and deal with issues that crop up. Failure to do so will tarnish your reputation and that of the project. This shouldn't deter you from contributing a library or application to the open source community, but it might—rightly so—cause you a moment's hesitation. Once you figure out the why, determine your level of commitment to publication, and decide what resources you're willing to commit.

Source as a Publication

You may not be thinking of shipping your project as publication; simply creating a public repo may be, you think, plenty. This can, however cause problems for your peers. GitHub is littered with a trail of cast-off toys in various states of disrepair. This kind of project serves to trip up those that follow behind, instead of providing enlightenment or purpose. Let's pinky-swear to be responsible adults, and take our published projects seriously.

The Clojure community in particular requires some nuance. It's a young community without a strong and established body of work. Clojure developers hunger for examples and support, so your contribution will garner more attention than Yet Another JavaScript Framework. The benefit is that a bunch of people are likely to look at your project. The drawback is exactly the same as the benefit. You shouldn't take this as a warning, but rather as a consideration.

Publication Platforms

Clojurists don't gather in a secret place to share their occult formulae. They publish to GitHub[1] or Bitbucket[2] like the rest of us. At present, far more projects live in GitHub than anywhere else, but use what works for you. Make sure your code can be seen by the audience you intend.

Setting up your source code to be viewable by the public is straightforward and varies by source control platform. Generally, it's push-button. Other concerns, however, shouldn't be overlooked. Let's consider licensing and collaboration.

Commonly, a bare source repo isn't enough. As a publisher, you may want features that help you manage your project or communicate with future collaborators. Several platforms include an issue tracker, a project wiki, download pages, and facilities for some variety of pull request. It's much easier to pick the right platform up front than to migrate later.

Beyond publication platform, you should also consider who can use your project and whether or not you want to encourage contribution.

---

1.   https://github.com
2.   https://bitbucket.org

Collaboration and Licensing

You should consider legal issues when publishing source code. Basically, this comes down to what rights you reserve for use and contribution. A reasonable synopsis of considerations can be found at choosealicense.com,[3] and many other online resources are available.

Clojure uses the Eclipse Public License v 1.0,[4] which allows authors of derivative works to use whatever license they choose. Many Clojure code bases (as well as other JVM languages' code bases) follow this pattern. Your choice of license will affect how the community receives your code base, the types of projects it's incorporated into, and the comfort level of companies that are considering it. A restrictive license will create a barrier to adoption and leave you with some legal duties enforcing the license. A more permissive license can be fire-and-forget.

If you're looking for collaborators, first consider whether you'll be employing a *contributor agreement* (CA). Clojure itself requires contributors to sign a contributor agreement,[5] a topic of regular discussion on the mailing list. A CA prevents contribution—that's its job—unless the contributor agrees to the terms, generally including protecting ownership, patent rights, licensing, and other concerns.

As with licensing, a number of resources are online for researching the legal issues around contribution and the ownership of open source projects. The Software Freedom Law Center provides an open source legal primer[6] as a starting place. For your responsibilities as a contributor, GitHub Guides has a nice overview for those getting started contributing to open source.[7]

You should also consider the *process* of collaboration. Will your contributors be using a pull request, a patch, or some other method of contributing? Will you merge in all changes yourself and require tests for each change, or hand out commit access like candy? If your code base gains wide adoption, you'll wish you had considered these questions up front; that's why we're pointing them out now.

Licensing and collaboration apply to published libraries and applications as well as public source repositories. Libraries require more effort to publish in a consumable way, as you'll see.

---

3. http://choosealicense.com
4. http://www.eclipse.org/legal/epl-v10.html
5. http://clojure.org/contributing
6. http://www.softwarefreedom.org/resources/2008/foss-primer.html
7. https://guides.github.com/activities/contributing-to-open-source/

Minimal Structure

The full contents of your source code repository will vary by project type, included languages, dependency-management system, and a host of other factors. But a few elements should be included in every repository so that a potential users or contributors can get their bearings.

At a minimum, your project needs a README file, a LICENSE file, and a CONTRIBUTING file.

README

The README file says what it does, and does what it says. Variations on this theme have historically included readme.1st, read.me, and a raft of variations and casing schemes. Whatever you call it, it should give your users a sense of the landscape.

The full contents of the README file can vary wildly, ranging from a change log with complete project history to documentation and tutorials. Regardless of what *else* you choose to put in this most fundamental document, you should include the following:

- What problem it solves—Tell the user why the project was started and what it accomplishes.

- How to get started—Document the steps to get the project up and running, or how to include or use it.

- An example—Give your users at least one demonstration of typical use.

- Oddness—Let the user know of anything that might violate the principle of least surprise.

- More information—List places the user can look for additional information should they need it.

LICENSE

The license that you've chosen should be documented at the top level of your repository in a LICENSE file. Including not only the text of the license but also a link to the canonical license is preferred. If using a versioned license, you should include the version of the license your project uses.

The LICENSE file can also include a copyright notice if you're choosing to maintain a copyright on the source code or documentation. Truly thorough authors (including the Clojure maintainers) prefer to keep the license and copyright information in the header of every file. In this case, a LICENSE file is probably unnecessary.

CONTRIBUTING

If you're accepting contributions, a CONTRIBUTING file should outline the rules for potential contributors. These include the submission method for contributions, file and code formats, testing requirements, documentation requirements, and any other criteria on which the contribution, patch, or pull request will be judged.

If your project requires a contributor agreement, the CONTRIBUTING file is the natural place for the text of the agreement and instructions on how to submit it. If it's an online form, a link to the form should be included.

Beyond publishing source code, you can opt to publish some form of binary. When publishing a library, bear in mind the guidelines for source publication, because they'll often apply.

Publishing Libraries

At some point your project may be ready for a library release, and it'll need someplace to go. Three main options present themselves: Clojars,[8] the Maven Central Repository (MCR)[9] (via one of approved hosting locations), or a self-hosted Maven repo. A good place to start reading is the Leiningen deployment documentation.[10]

Clojars provides for a straightforward publication with minimal fuss. Clojars has two repositories: Classic and Release. Classic is the Wild West, having almost no restrictions. Release requires that the library be *in good order*—versioned, described, and signed. Both options require an account and some fairly minimal configuration.

If you're looking for a little more reach—especially if you're targeting the Java community—the MCR serves a broader audience. This comes at a cost, however: the MCR is definitely not the Wild West. Perhaps the easiest way to get your libraries and artifacts into the MCR is the Sonatype OSS Repository,[11] which accepts any open source software artifacts.

Finally, you can set up and maintain your own Maven repository. You might want to do this to track downloads or to restrict access. The simplest case may be to set up an AWS S3 bucket, then use s3-wagon-private[12] by Phil Hagelberg. For a more advanced configuration, you have some reading to do.

---

8. https://clojars.org/
9. http://maven.apache.org/repository/index.html
10. https://github.com/technomancy/leiningen/blob/preview/doc/DEPLOY.md
11. http://nexus.sonatype.org/oss-repository-hosting.html
12. https://github.com/technomancy/s3-wagon-private

Documentation

It's hard to take full advantage of a source base or library that's nothing more than code. The early Clojure community had a reputation—perhaps deservedly so—for terrible documentation. This is slowly changing, and many current projects provide good getting-started pages, API guides, examples, and walkthroughs.

For a smaller library, a well-constructed README file can suffice. For larger projects, consider adding a documentation site of some sort (for example, a GitHub wiki). Large projects would also do well to include some examples and an introduction for new users. Beyond a certain size or user base, an announcement mailing list and even a blog can be appropriate.

Ask yourself a few questions. Will a new user know how to use my project? Where will the users go to find information about my project? Does my project have any unintuitive features, or features that are likely to be misunderstood or cause frustration? Your documentation should resolve these concerns.

Marketing and Maintenance

Marketing? Yes. Your release is a product, and if you treat it like a product, marketed to its intended audience, you'll get users, collaborators, decent press, and a groundswell of support. Do this wrong, and you'll at best be ignored and at worst look downright silly.

When you're ready to announce, do so on commonly viewed channels. You're probably already a member of the Clojure Google Group.[13] The group provides the right audience for a source or library release. Include a description and how to get started and links to the documentation, and be ready for questions. Additionally, a blog post about your release with a brief introduction and some sample code posted to Planet Clojure[14] (or another aggregator) will also spread the word. In both of these cases, the important questions to clearly answer are: what problem does this solve? and, when should I use this tool?

Be prepared for questions, comments, and a community to support. You need a feedback mechanism; maybe the comment section of your announcement post, or a dedicated email address *that you actually check*, or perhaps GitHub Issues[15] or JIRA.[16] Be a responsible product owner, not an absentee landlord.

---

13. https://groups.google.com/forum/#!forum/clojure
14. http://planet.clojure.in/
15. https://github.com/features#issues
16. https://www.atlassian.com/software/jira

Finally, when you're no longer maintaining the project, make that clear. You can hand it off to another maintainer, add a notice to the documentation that the project is unmaintained, or shut things down entirely.

Source code and libraries, once published, tend to be static artifacts. On the other hand, deployed applications must account for the needs and configuration of the environments to which they're deployed. Let's take a look our options for getting an application live.

Choose a Deployment Environment

Some applications are intended to be run locally, either on the desktop or at the command line. In Clojure, these applications are distributed as libraries or source repositories. Network-aware applications, in contrast, run in remote environments. When considering the deployment of a network application, you have a lot of information to choose from. Private or public? Platform or infrastructure? Managed application server or daemon? Clojure applications are no different.

Let's walk through these options at a high level; we'll start with an overview, then explore deployments with two platforms (Heroku and AWS Elastic Beanstalk). Next we'll deploy using an application server, wrapping up with some guidelines for building your own deployment environment. As the decisions become more complex, we'll drop from specifics to generalized advice, but by the end of this chapter, you'll have a few solid jumping-off points for the deployment of your Clojure application.

Find a Home: Public or Private?

The first question to ask yourself is, what environment will my application live in? The answer may have design implications that should be considered before you undertake any development. Let's take a quick walking tour of the options and some of the considerations that might lead you in one direction or another.

If you're a startup or small business with little to no technical infrastructure, a public cloud service is an attractive option. The early investment required for a presence in the public cloud is close to nothing, and many services provide some facilities to aid in scaling the application both horizontally and vertically. If you're working within a startup or small business, you'll find *Deploy to a Platform*, on page 185 valuable.

A large (or well-funded) organization may have invested time, money, and other resources into building its own private data center. If the organization is already heavily committed to the JVM, you may be deploying into an existing application server (for example, WebSphere or WildFly). Otherwise, you'll want to provision one yourself. If that's the case, *Deployment to an Application Server*, on page 194 will guide you through that process.

Either group may find that a stand-alone service suits its needs more effectively than a platform or a provisioned application server. Developers creating a stand-alone services can find help in *Running as a Service*, on page 193.

Organizations with internal data centers can still benefit from using the public cloud; a harried operations team may appreciate your prototyping in the public cloud, giving them time to get up to speed on the desired private production environment.

Whether your organization is large or fledgling, one of the main trade-offs to make is determining who's in control of your uptime. In using public services, we're depending on our cloud services provider to keep things running and connected. As they've matured, existing cloud providers' infrastructures have become increasingly reliable, but for applications that offer a service-level agreement to its users, giving up control of uptime is a major risk.

Some things to think about when choosing among public providers are:

- Does scaling happen automatically? What are the service's scalability limits?

- Are there any limits on network traffic or storage, and when would we expect to reach them? What do overages cost?

- How well will the network handle a distributed denial-of-service (DDOS) attack, or even a sound slashdotting?

- What facilities are present for disaster recovery?

- What will its lifetime cost be? Some services' rates can increase steeply when scaling out.

- How easy is it to transfer data in and out of the service?

In the public space, you can break your decision down further, depending on the scope of your application and how much control you need.

Consider the Cloud

It's easy to forget how long the cloud has been around in some form or another. VMware had been selling virtualization software for private hardware for nearly a decade when Clojure's first release arrived in 2007. In that same year, Amazon's Elastic Cloud Computing service was undergoing its public beta. Clojure evolved in a world where our current notions about cloud computing had already taken root, and it was designed with cloud computing in mind.

Let's take a look at the two types of cloud environments we're likely to employ and when each environment serves our needs best. Our options are many; by understanding their trade-offs, we can make sound choices about our deployment environment.

Platforms as a Service

A Platform as a Service (PaaS) provides an environment that your application can be deployed into, largely without considering the particulars of server or network configuration, scalability, or storage. If you're building a prototype, or a simple application needing little more than an execution environment and access to a data store, PaaS may be just the thing.

This choice comes with some limitations, however. You must play by the rules of the sandbox's owner. Not only are you giving up control of our connectivity and choice of environment, but you also give up some process management options. This can be a good or a bad thing, depending on your application.

Other PaaS considerations include:

- *How easy is easy?* As your application incorporates less standard behavior, you'll begin to shift focus away from platforms and into stand-alone services or another custom solution. As a rule of thumb, if the configuration changes (or the cost for supplementary services) start to outweigh the benefit, consider building your own service.

- *What are its rules for recovery and restart?* If your application requires resiliency, you should ensure that the platform you're deploying to will recover from errors. If your application needs to be highly available, for instance, you'll want some redundancy. That means a platform like Elastic Beanstalk that allows for automated scalability and load balancing.

- *What logging and monitoring services are available?* You should be able to store log entries in an easily retrievable format for as long as you're likely to need them. If you're updating weekly, you'll only need a week's worth of storage. If less frequently, more storage may be required. Be sure to log at a level that will allow you do debug any problems.

- *How granular or configurable is the service's notification system?* Will it send you an email on a critical error? A text message? Does the service allow you to access its notification system from within the application? Decide what level of notification you want and what level of urgency a type of notification requires, and ensure that the platform you're looking at can accommodate you.

In the next section, we'll consider two PaaS providers: Heroku and AWS Elastic Beanstalk. The many others include Jelastic, Openshift, Cloudbees, and Google AppEngine.

Infrastructure as a Service

Infrastructure as a Service (IaaS) allows us more flexibility to create environments customized to our needs, but the customization isn't without cost. Depending on the service, we may need to start from a bare operating system and install and configure everything atop it. In an IaaS scenario, we'll need to add environmental provisioning and configuration to our application. AWS and Rackspace are the heavy hitters in this category, but many options exist.

Although we get control of our execution environment, we're still dependent on our IaaS provider for our uptime and connectivity. We're trading control and effort. To get a measure of control, we sacrifice time spent on operational concerns. Most of the provisioning can be automated, but choosing IaaS leads to a number of other choices.

If your application needs more than just a process, a network connection, and a data store, IaaS will likely be your public cloud choice. This is particularly true if it has an unusual or nonstandard configuration or requires detailed and near-realtime monitoring.

Other IaaS considerations include:

- *How configurable is the network topology?* Spinning up virtual machines (VMs) on the fly is all well and good, but your ideal network architecture may require multiple tiers, each with more restrictive access. Ensure that the IaaS will be as configurable as you need it to be.

- *Are my VMs sequestered from other VMs in the same cloud?* You may have security concerns that require running in an environment with some degree of network privacy. Some IaaS providers do this by default; others require configuration.

- *Can credentials be shared? How granular is the provider's authentication system?* The larger your organization, the more people will be touching any given project's infrastructure. Odds are good you'll want separate authentication and authorization for every person.

- *Can I distribute my application across facilities? Power grids? States? Countries?* High-availability apps may want geographical redundancy as well as logical redundancy, or network and power redundancy inside the same facility. Ensuring that uptime isn't compromised during a network failure, power failure, or meteor strike may be important. If so, pay attention to the location of the IaaS provider's data centers.

- *How do I connect the cloud portion of my application back to my corporate VPN?* Both Amazon (Virtual Private Cloud)[17] and RackSpace (RackConnect)[18] offer services that allow the extension of a VPN into their cloud environments. A hybrid cloud is a good option for gaining scalable infrastructure that doesn't require investing additional capital in your organization's data center.

This list of considerations is hardly comprehensive but should give you a strong start in deciding among IaaS providers.

This section has covered PaaS and IaaS at a high level, but we should look at the specifics of deployment to a platform before making decisions.

Deploy to a Platform

A platform-based app deployment can be a great option if you want to get started providing simple apps and services quickly. They are cost-effective, scale easily, and provide most common services that a simple application will require. When combined with other services (such as DNS and storage services), a PaaS can eliminate the need for administration of the underlying operating system.

Of course, with a PaaS, our application is limited to the services available in the provider's sandbox. If our system grows and more control over the details of the environment become necessary, we'll need to migrate away from our PaaS provider. We'll look at two PaaS providers: Heroku and Amazon's Elastic Beanstalk.

Deploying to Heroku

Heroku was founded in 2007 as a platform for deploying applications in Ruby. Since that time, it has added support for a number of other languages, including a solid commitment to Clojure. Deploying a Clojure application is a straightforward process with solid documentation.

---

17. http://docs.aws.amazon.com/AmazonVPC/latest/UserGuide/VPC_VPN.html
18. http://www.rackspace.com/cloud/hybrid/rackconnect/

Design Considerations

A Clojure application intended for deployment to Heroku has only a few additional concerns. First, any dynamic configuration should be read from environment variables. This includes any secure information we don't want to store in our source control repository, such as auth information, AWS credentials, per-environment database authentication, and similar information. Second, understand that Heroku won't allow us to write to disk. Uploading files or logging will need to be accomplished in another fashion.

One common place for file storage from an application deployed to Heroku is Amazon's Simple Storage Service (S3). James Reeves has written a Clojure library for this very thing.[19]

Basic Deployment

We'll be using Git to deploy to Heroku, but first we'll need to set a few things up. We should already have our app directory set up as a Git repo (git init), because Heroku will require a git remote.

We'll need a Heroku account and an app we can deploy to. It's possible to configure everything from Heroku's website. However, Heroku provides a command-line application called the Heroku Toolbelt[20] that simplifies much of the work. Having installed the toolbelt, we create the app from the console:

```
heroku apps:create [our-app-name]
```

We'll deploy the app by pushing to a git remote. Using the Toolbelt will set that remote for us. If we created the app using the website, we'd need to set that by hand:

```
git remote add heroku git@heroku.com:our-app-name.git
```

The Toolbelt also creates a Procfile for us, in our project's root. This file will be used to start the processes on Heroku. It contains the following:

```
web: lein with-profile production trampoline run -m our-app-name.web
```

In short, it says to start the web process with lein using those options.

Once all of our configuration has been set, we're ready to deploy our app by pushing a branch to heroku:

```
git push heroku master
```

Once our app is deployed, we can visit it at http://our-app-name.herokuapp.com.

---

19. http://github.com/weavejester/clj-aws-s3
20. http://toolbelt.heroku.com

lein-heroku

Phil Hagelberg has created a lein template[21] for use with Heroku that provides a little grease for the wheels. When you're creating a web application from scratch, it's an excellent resource.

Select a Data Store

Through Heroku's add-ons, many databases are available for use. PostgreSQL remains a popular choice; it's been around the longest (on Heroku) and has the most support. In addition, add-ons for Redis, Memcached, MongoDB, and a plethora of others are available. Choose a data store from among the list of add-ons, and it'll be available for your application to connect to.

To communicate with your data store, you'll need to pass its location and credentials to your application. We discuss this in more depth in Chapter 9, *Formatting Data*, on page 157; if you skipped over that chapter on your way here, you may want to review. To get that information to your app, you'll need to do some configuration.

Manage Your Configuration

When we develop apps with volatile configuration, a reasonable practice is to store that configuration in an environment variable. Although we still have the option to read data into our application from .properties files, we may have information that we don't want stored in source control. For instance, if we were configuring our application with single-user basic authentication, we might build a function like this:

```
(defn- authenticated? [user pass]
  (= [user pass] [(System/getenv "AUTH_USER") (System/getenv "AUTH_PASS")])))
```

Don't look at us like that. We've all done it. But in a production app, we shouldn't be storing our authentication information in a plain-text environment variable, or using basic authentication.[22] You'll be using multiple users and hashed and salted passwords. You'll still need to store some sensitive information somewhere the application can find it. By retrieving sensitive information from the environment, you obviate the need to store it on a file system somewhere where prying eyes can see it even more easily. (*System Configuration*, on page 131 includes information on two environment-management libraries you might find useful here.)

---

21. https://github.com/technomancy/lein-heroku
22. http://en.wikipedia.org/wiki/Basic_access_authentication

Another commonly stored configuration element for web apps running on Heroku is the database's connection string:

```
(ns app-with-db
  (:require [clojure.java.jdbc :as db]))

(defn do-something [data]
  (db/with-connection (System/getenv "DATABASE_URL")
  «do something with data»
  ))
```

With Heroku, that practice is strongly encouraged. Not only does that give us the flexibility to change our configuration without redeploying, but Heroku keeps a history of our configuration changes for us, should we lose our minds.

Different add-ons will provision different environment variables for connection strings. To keep things consistent, Heroku recommends using DATABASE_URL across the board in single-database applications.

To retrieve an app's full configuration, run heroku config. If we were looking for our PostgreSQL config, for instance, we might run:

```
heroku config | grep POSTGRES
# -> HEROKU_POSTGRESQL_COLOR_URL: postgres://user:pw@dbhost.com:5432/dbname
```

A couple of interesting configuration options are available for Clojure (or Java) apps running on Heroku. In addition to DATABASE_URL, we can set MVN_OPTS, JAVA_OPTS, and any other environment variables lein will use (for example, LEIN_NO_DEV). These options can be set with heroku config:add. For instance, to set our JVM options, we do this:

```
heroku config:add JVM_OPTS='-Xmx768m -XX:+SomeOtherOption'
```

Scaling Heroku

Heroku apps run on a process model. A *process* refers to a single JVM running on a managed process called a *dyno*. A process can be a web process, a console process, a scheduled task, or anything requiring computing resources. Each one runs in its own managed process. Our web application will run in a web process, with most other tasks running in a worker process. Scaling our app happens in the context of these dynos.

We can scale our application to a limited degree vertically, and much more freely horizontally.

In the vertical direction, we can increase the size of our dyno; a 1X dyno (the default) consists of 512MB of memory and 1x CPU share per dyno. If an app requires a little more horsepower, this can be increased to a 2X dyno, which

Sharing a Database Among Services

Since we're already populating DATABASE_URL with the value of our connection string, it becomes easy to share our database connection information among running apps. Retrieve the connection string from the app with the appropriate add-on, and set it in any other app sharing that database.

doubles both CPU and memory. If that's not enough for your workhorse process, too bad.

Horizontally, you have more options. If you've designed your app with this in mind, you can run many web processes (or any other processes) concurrently. This won't help with bottlenecks in other places (the database, for example), and it can exacerbate the problem, so we hope you were paying attention in Chapter 5, *Use Your Cores*, on page 85.

Also, each process will be running in its own JVM. Although what you do within your JVM is your own business, communicating among those processes requires an outside agency. The default limit for a single process type is 100 dynos, with more available upon request. In a well-designed application, a lot of work can get done.

To scale our application, we are once again presented with the Heroku website or the Toolbelt. Using the Toolbelt, we can change the size of our dyno with ps:resize:

```
heroku ps:resize web=2X worker=1X
```

To change the number of dynos, we use ps:scale:

```
heroku ps:scale web=4
```

Changing these settings will restart all of the affected processes.

Mind Your JVM

Changing from a 1X to a 2X dyno doesn't reset the JVM options to the appropriate levels; it makes more memory available to the process, but the memory limits of the JVM are still governed by the JVM_OPTS setting.

Logging and Monitoring on Heroku

Heroku doesn't allow processes to create files. How, then—logging? The things we'd normally be logging are output to STDOUT and STDERR in our process. (Want a look at the running log? Run heroku logs -t.) We can send our internal logging elsewhere, or take advantage of a number of logging-related add-ons[23] that connect to our Heroku application.

Monitoring concerns both uptime and performance. Uptime is reported from Heroku, but that's not going to give us the complete picture. Likewise, Pingdom[24] and similar services can provide a periodic check but fail to exercise the entire application. They're still useful, but any real performance analysis requires deeper integration.

Many developers have found success using New Relic. New Relic provides an add-on Java agent you can include from your project.clj file that will instrument and monitor the performance of your application. We can add this to our application by including New Relic's Java agent in our JVM_OPTS:

```
$ heroku config:add JVM_OPTS='[other_options] -javaagent:newrelic/newrelic.jar'
```

Additional details can be found at New Relic's documentation site.[25]

Though diagnosing an application failure is beyond the scope of this book, testing prior to release combined with performance monitoring and logging will provide a good starting place for investigating future problems.

Deploy to AWS Elastic Beanstalk

Whether AWS Elastic Beanstalk (EB) is a PaaS or a thin set of conveniences over other AWS offerings is the subject of some debate. For our purposes, we'll treat it as though it's a platform, even though it doesn't offer some of the same conveniences as Heroku.

EB has been live since January 2011, supporting Java deployment from day one. Though EB doesn't support Clojure explicitly, it's become a popular choice for deploying Clojure applications. When it's viewed as a part of the AWS landscape, a dizzying array of options for file and data storage, scalability, and network configuration become available. We'll focus on the particulars of EB itself.

Design Considerations

Deploying to EB raises a few of the same concerns as Heroku. Dynamic configuration (such as the database connection string) should be read from environment variables. We'll talk more about configuration in a moment.

---

23. https://addons.heroku.com/#logging
24. http://pingdom.com
25. https://docs.newrelic.com/docs/java/the-new-relic-java-agent-and-security

Unlike Heroku, EB allows access to the file system. It's not suitable for long-term storage or permanent files, however: EB will boot up an AWS Elastic Compute Cloud (EC2) instance with your app installed, and the file system in question will be ephemeral. Files intended to be permanent should be stored elsewhere, and data that needs to be durable should be placed in a data store or in S3. Temp files are fine, however.

If configured with autoscaling, EB will start and stop instances as demand requires. Because of this, the app you intend to deploy mustn't depend on manual configuration after the application starts.

Basic Deployment

With Heroku, we used the Git tool to deploy; with AWS Elastic Beanstalk, we'll use lein, specifically James Reeves' lein-beanstalk plugin.[26] The instructions provided in the README.md are pretty sound.

First, we need to set up an AWS account and activate EB. Then we add our AWS credentials to our lein initialization at ~/.lein/init.clj:

```
(def lein-beanstalk-credentials
  {:access-key "ACCESS_KEY"
   :secret-key "SECRET"})
```

Once that's in order, we can deploy our application using lein:

```
$ lein beanstalk deploy development
Created project_directory/target/project-1.0.0-SNAPSHOT-20140328082105.war
Uploaded project-1.0.0-SNAPSHOT-20140328082105.war to S3 Bucket
Created new app version 1.0.0-SNAPSHOT-20140328082105
Creating 'development' environment (this may take several minutes)
..................................... Done
Environment deployed at: project-dev.elasticbeanstalk.com
```

After our app is deployed, we can visit it at the address noted in the output from lein.

Set Up a Data Store

EB doesn't have a data store as readily accessible as Heroku. Getting an application deployed creates more work, but you can configure any data store you want. Amazon provides several options (RDS, ElastiCache, DynamoDB, and so on). Instead, you can configure a custom service on an EC2 instance, or even something external to AWS, provided that data store allows access from EB.

---

26. https://github.com/weavejester/lein-beanstalk

Configuration

The EB platform provides a plethora of configuration options[27]—many more than we could possible cover in a single chapter. These configuration options can be varied by environment and are set through an entry in your project.clj file:

```
:aws
  {:beanstalk
   {:environments
    [{:name "staging"
      :cname-prefix "myapp-staging"
      ;; additional staging env options
      :env {"DATABASE_URL" "mysql://..."}}
     {:name "load-test"
      :cname-prefix "myapp-load"
      ;; additional load env options
      :env {"DATABASE_URL" "mysql://..."}}]}}
```

Scaling EB

If your application requires scaling, you can configure your environment with an AutoScale Group[28] and an Elastic Load Balancer.[29] You can set these services up either through the web console, or from your application's configuration.

Logging and Monitoring

EB allows inspection of the application and environment logs in two ways. From the EB console, you can request a snapshot of the log file. You can also configure an S3 bucket to receive the logs generated by your application.[30]

When you run any application on AWS—including EB—metrics and monitoring from CloudWatch are available. When deploying a single instance, you can enable instance-level monitoring. When you create an AutoScale Group or use Elastic Load Balancing, individual monitoring can also be aggregated across the group.

Provision Your Own Servers

PaaS offerings are convenient, but they can't always handle the requirements of an application's ecosystem. If your organization has a standing data center, convincing the product owner that the best option for deployment is PaaS in

---

27. http://docs.aws.amazon.com/elasticbeanstalk/latest/dg/command-options.html
28. http://aws.amazon.com/documentation/autoscaling/
29. http://aws.amazon.com/documentation/elasticloadbalancing/
30. http://docs.aws.amazon.com/elasticbeanstalk/latest/dg/using-features.loggingS3.title.html

the cloud *probably* won't fly. Similarly, many organizations maintaining sensitive data tend to avoid deployment on public hardware. If you've designed an application that's highly concurrent, the available cloud offerings may not provide you with enough cores. Many, many circumstances exist in which we may need or prefer to configure our own platform.

Let's explore our other options for deployment. Although this isn't intended to be a comprehensive operational overview, when you leave this chapter you should be aware of all the major options for deploying your Clojure application into a custom-built environment.

We'll start with running an application as a stand-alone service, then have a look at deploying to a Java application server. Finally, we'll make some recommendations for choosing a deployment setup for use inside your company's data center. When we're done, you should have the tools to either set up an environment yourself or to have a serious conversation with the operations staff about what you'll need.

Running as a Service

While in development, you were probably using lein run to start and test your application. If we're deploying our application as a stand-alone service, it'll need to be able to run using only java. This requires a few extra steps. We'll be generating an uberjar using lein uberjar, so we'll need to set our :uberjar options in our project.clj file. These options should instruct lein to create classes ahead-of-time (AOT) where appropriate, and should include an application server in its dependencies. Jetty works well for this, since it's lightweight. You can also use :main to specify the location of the method that kicks off the server. This makes for a cleaner command-line start.

If we were writing a Pedestal[31] application, that setup would look something like this:

```
(defproject my-service "0.0.3-SNAPSHOT"
  :description "a simple web service"
  ; ...
  :uberjar {:main [my-service.server]
            :aot :all
            :dependencies [[io.pedestal/pedestal.jetty "0.2.2"]]})
```

You would then create the JAR and run it with java:

```
$ lein uberjar
$ java -jar target/my-service-0.0.3-SNAPSHOT-standalone.jar
```

---

31. http://pedestal.io

Your application will be up and running on port 8080.

On your server, you'd configure this just like any other service; in Linux, this would mean creating a daemon config file, assigning it to a run level, and adding it to the init process. Once it's configured, you manage the service like any other web application.

If this sounds like a lot of work and configuration, it is. The resulting service, however, only has one dependency: java itself. This can be an appealing option for a one-off application, or to run within a production environment already providing several services.

More commonly, we can deploy to an already-configured servlet container such as Jetty or Tomcat. Let's give that a go.

Deployment to an Application Server

Deploying your Clojure application to a Java application server—less formally known as a servlet container—is often more convenient than configuring, securing, managing, and monitoring each service individually. These containers can have many advanced features, scale well, and can (if properly configured) improve resource utilization across an organization. If this is familiar territory, you may want to skip ahead. Otherwise, we'll give you a brief tour of the application server landscape and show you how to deploy your applications into these services. Whether you are taking advantage of your company's data center or building a server (or cluster) in a cloud-based IaaS platform, understanding the application servers will be useful.

Deployment

Too many electrons have given their lives in debates over what constitutes a Java application server and in defending an author's or developer's personal favorite. We won't be getting into this. Currently Tomcat is the most prevalent application server in the wild. Worthy competitors are Jetty and JBoss AS (now called WildFly), with a few others making blips on the radar.

If your organization is significantly invested in JVM languages, odds are good the choice of application server has already been made, and virtual machines ready for launch are standing by waiting for the go order.

Thankfully, deployment to any of these platforms is similar. Provided you've configured your server to scan for hot deployments, deploying your web application is a matter of depositing a WAR file (alternatively, an EAR file in the case of WildFly) in the right directory. The application server scans that directory at a configurable interval and will pick up the change during the next scan.

Servlet Containers vs. JEE App Servers

It's worth mentioning here that servlet containers (such as Tomcat) provide just enough functionality to serve a web application from a WAR file. A Java Enterprise Edition (JEE) application server (such as WildFly) provides a raft of additional functionality. WildFly includes a Java Message Service (JMS) messaging provider, transaction management, clustering, and many other enterprise features.

If your application uses these features, a JEE container must be used. If not—and if you have no plans to include them in the future—then all of this extra, unused functionality is merely going to slow you down.

In Tomcat[32] and Jetty,[33] you deploy to the /webapps/ directory in their respective homes. Place the .WAR file in the directory and you're good to go.

WildFly requires an additional step.[34] The deployment directory can be found at $JBOSS_HOME/standalone/deployments/. Once you've uploaded the application container file, you need to add a file marker to indicate that the server should deploy the application. The filename of the marker file is the same as the file to deploy with .dodeploy added to the end. For example, if you were pushing my-web-app.war, you would also push my-web-app.war.dodeploy into the deployment directory.

Immutant

The Immutant[a] project takes a swing at reducing incidental complexity for projects looking to use the features of JBoss Application Server version 7.[b] Immutant 1.x provides support for Clojure applications that want to use AS7's included features, packaging them with the application server for ease of development and deployment.

In April 2015, the Immutant team released Immutant 2.x, called the deuce. This effort effectively unwraps the container and provides Clojure applications with libraries that include container features as needed. It's early yet, but it's a project worth checking out.

---

a.   http://immutant.org/
b.   http://jbossas.jboss.org/

---

32. http://tomcat.apache.org/tomcat-8.0-doc/deployer-howto.html
33. http://www.eclipse.org/jetty/documentation/current/hot-deployment.html
34. https://docs.jboss.org/author/display/WFLY8/Application+deployment

Building an Environment

If you're building a Clojure deployment environment from scratch, you'll need to choose how that application server environment (or those environments!) is configured. Each option has its advantages and trade-offs. You should do your own homework here, but consider the following questions:

- How difficult is it to install/maintain?

- What's the community like? Will it be easy to find advice?

- Is it well-documented?

- What is its performance profile?

- How configurable is it?

- How much does it cost?

- What licenses does it operate under?

- Is it elastic and scalable? Does it support clustering?

- How robust is the tooling around the server? Are plugins or add-ons available?

Once you've compared the answers to those questions against your organization's needs, pick the platform that meets those needs best. We'll offer some general advice here, however.

For low-to-medium-volume applications that need to run in isolation, either embedding Jetty in your application, or deploying to a Jetty server dedicated to the application, yields a good balance between lightweight and well-performing—with a minimum of management overhead. You can deploy this configuration to a minimally provisioned host.

If you're launching a high-value, high-traffic application, dedicate a cluster to the application. This'll give you the availability and scalability this type of application requires. You'll also benefit from the monitoring and security features a clusterable application server typically includes. In exchange for these features and robustness, you'll need to plan your environment more carefully.

Finally, consider setting up a hatchery—an incubation environment for many applications that are either small or still in development. You'll be able to manage each application individually using the cluster's tools, without provisioning multiple environments. This'll give you solid resource utilization and a boost to project startup times.

Wrapping Up

We hope you've enjoyed this whirlwind tour of publishing and deployment options, and are only a little bit dizzy. By now, you should be aware of the options and responsibilities relating to publishing your source and distributing your libraries. We've also pointed out a number of landmarks in the landscape of application deployment. Let's review.

Whether you're publishing source or distributing libraries, you should examine your motivations for publication, ensure that your feedback mechanisms will serve the community and your adopters, carefully consider your licensing options, and document your work. Treat your publication like any other: market well, announce to the right audience, and then do your best to keep your customers (the folks using your source and libraries) happy.

Deploying to a cloud platform provides a certain level of convenience but potentially limits the size of—and the toys in—your sandbox (in the case of Heroku), and requires a commitment to a third-party vendor's offerings (in the case of EB). In both cases, be aware of your eventual needs, and take sensible steps to avoid painting yourself into a corner.

Deploying an application to an application server, or including an application server in with your application, yields a high degree of control and takes advantage of your organization's sunk costs.[35] Application servers also provide a number of interesting features you may want or need. Running your own system, however, comes with the usual administrative overhead and may not be as flexible or ephemeral as you want.

Bearing all this in mind, build some applications, and show us what you've learned.

---

35. http://en.wikipedia.org/wiki/Sunk_costs

Roots

Almost nothing in Clojure is new. Quite the opposite—some of Clojure's ideas are very old. It may seem to be a fledgling language when stacked against Java, C++, and other high-mileage languages, but don't let the new-car smell fool you. When Rich Hickey wrote Clojure, he did so using mature ideas and sound theories.

Let's explore the language's history, observing those principles at ground zero. Set the dial on your way-back machine to 1936.

Reasonability

Clojure really begins to take a shape we would recognize in the *American Journal of Mathematics*. Alonzo Church published *An Unsolvable Problem of Elementary Number Theory [Chu36]*,[1] establishing the principles of the *untyped lambda calculus*.

The lambda calculus or (λ-calculus) is a formal system for representing computational structures as functions with variables bound to inputs and substituted when the function is evaluated.

The lambda calculus provides a formal notation for *functions*, including *recursive and anonymous functions*. In the text, functions were considered *first-order objects*, and *higher-order functions*—functions that return functions as output—are described. These concepts are fundamental to Clojure and other function-oriented languages. The notation allowed then-mathematicians to represent computational structures using a shared language that could be reasoned about.

---

1.   http://phil415.pbworks.com/f/Church.pdf

A programming language wouldn't take advantage of the lambda calculus for more than two decades.

Lisp

John McCarthy published *Recursive Functions of Symbolic Expressions and Their Computation by Machine, Part I [McC60]* in the April 1960 edition of *Communications of the ACM (CACM)*, describing the development of the Lisp system by the Artificial Intelligence group at the Massachusetts Institute of Technology.[2] Lisp's general structure took its cues from the lambda calculus.

McCarthy and his team included Church's notions of anonymous functions, functions as first- and higher-order structures. They also extended the lambda-calculus's propositional and predicate functions (true, false, and, or, not, and other logic) into *conditional expressions*, making it easy to compute a recursive function without falling into an infinite loop. Lisp also implemented *garbage collection*.

Perhaps most important, Lisp was designed around the idea of *code as data*. The fundamental unit of code in Lisp is the *symbolic expression* (s-expression). These can be collected into self-referencing *labeled functions* (*s-functions*). These are simply data structures, and they can be operated on like any other data structure. This idea was powerful and facilitated metaprogramming.

The Lisp syntax and its included functions and data structures were limited, by design. Between 1960 and 2005, many implementations of Lisp expanded on these original ideas, giving Common Lisp and Clojure much of its current shape while keeping its core small.

Macros and Metaprogramming

In the same issue of *CACM*, a short-lived extensible-languages movement was kicked off by M. Douglas McIlroy with *Macro Instruction Extensions of Compiler Languages [McI60]*.[3] Given Lisp's sparse syntax and limited core feature set—and corresponding appetite for language extension—it was natural that three years later Timothy Hart would propose *macros* for addition to Lisp.[4]

Since Lisp code is also data, its users were already metaprogramming. The addition of macros after Lisp 1.5 added a macro-expansion phase to the interpretation of Lisp programs, giving things roughly the shape we see today.

---

2.   http://www-formal.stanford.edu/jmc/recursive.html

3.   http://dl.acm.org/citation.cfm?id=367223

4.   ftp://publications.ai.mit.edu/ai-publications/pdf/AIM-057.pdf

Macros provided for a faster path for programmers to extend Lisp. They could redefine core features on not much more than a whim without cluttering up the core language at all.

Enough about the language core and its extensibility. Let's talk data.

Persistent Data Structures

Clojure's core functionality focuses on *immutable values*, emphasizing the functional approach of consuming a value and returning a new, updated value. This facilitates concurrency, because the old value can be viewed by another thread without vanishing or updating unpredictably. To both approach immutability and create "new" values efficiently, these values are implemented as *persistent data structures*.

This idea was first fully realized by Driscoll, Sarnak, Sleator, and Tarjan in a 1986 paper *Making Data Structures Persistent [DSST89]* in the *Journal of Computer and Systems Sciences*.[5] Naturally, it drew on dozens of other sources and prior publications. The paper covered many different techniques by which persistence can be achieved and defined the nomenclature.

The Clojure persistent vector and map are Hash Array Mapped Tries and descend directly from Phil Bagwell's work on ideal hash trees.[6] Immutability is such an important foundation for Clojure that it's impossible to imagine Clojure without them. These data structures are the key that makes immutability efficient enough to work.

Lazy and Delayed Evaluation

Laziness refers to the delay in the evaluation of an expression until it's required. In many of Clojure's evaluation algorithms, data structures are abstracted as logical lists or *sequences*. Sequencing enables the *lazy evaluation* of the sequence's elements, realizing performance gains in many circumstances and allowing for the creation of infinite lists.

Peter Henderson and James H. Morris, Jr. introduced *A Lazy Evaluator [HM76]*[7] to Lisp in 1976, building on the call-by-need mechanism introduced by Wadsworth in *Semantics and Pragmatics of the Lambda-calculus [Wad71]* and

---

5. http://www.cs.cmu.edu/~sleator/papers/another-persistence.pdf
6. http://infoscience.epfl.ch/record/64398/files/idealhashtrees.pdf
7. http://dl.acm.org/citation.cfm?id=811543

the *delay* rule as presented by Jean Vuillemin in *Correct and Optimal Implementations of Recursion in a Simple Programming Language [Vui73].*[8]

In addition to lazy evaluation by default in many features, Clojure also includes the delay macro for deferring evaluation. Note that delay isn't asynchronous; it simply delays synchronous evaluation until later.

Futures and Promises

For *asynchronous evaluation*, Clojure's core features include the future, proposed by Baker and Dewitt in *The Incremental Garbage Collection of Processes [HB77][9]* as a means of concurrent evaluation in 1977. The promise, facilitating synchronization of concurrent threads, is also provided. Promises were proposed in 1976 by Friedman and Wise in their paper *The Impact of Applicative Programming on Multiprocessing [FW76].* Both futures and promises enjoy widespread implementation in both functional and object-oriented languages.

These aren't the only concurrency mechanisms currently available. Clojure added the core.async contrib library to supplement its concurrency toolkit in 2013.

Concurrent Channels

With core.async Clojure includes the notion of *channels*. This line of thought began life with Sir C. A. R. Hoare in *Communicating Sequential Processes [Hoa78],*[10] but the theory was expanded into a much more complete form in 1984.[11]

Channels add to Clojure's concurrency support by providing thread-independent activity queues through which processes can communicate. It cleanly solves the information-exchange problems that have spawned mechanisms like callbacks and observers.

Multiversion Concurrency Control

In 1978, David Patrick Reed published *Naming and Synchronization in a Decentralized Computer System [Ree78][12]* describing *multiversion concurrency control* (MVCC). This idea was expanded upon in *Concurrency Control in*

---

8. http://dl.acm.org/citation.cfm?id=804054
9. http://dl.acm.org/citation.cfm?id=806932
10. http://dl.acm.org/citation.cfm?id=359585
11. http://dl.acm.org/citation.cfm?doid=828.833
12. http://publications.csail.mit.edu/lcs/pubs/pdf/MIT-LCS-TR-205.pdf

Distributed Database Systems [BG81][13] by Phillip Bernstein and Nathan Goodman in 1981.

Their ideas form the basis of Clojure's implementation of software transactional memory (STM), a critical element in Clojure's concurrency toolbox.

That concludes our brief survey of the roots of Clojure and the inspiration for many of its headliners. It's easy to see that Rich Hickey made intentional, well-reasoned choices when creating Clojure.

Wrapping Up

There's wisdom in history. Hickey and his collaborators were able to create a thoughtful, well-reasoned language because they knew this history and could apply its wisdom.

In our industry, we don't focus much on our roots and core principles outside of formal education in mathematics or computer science. We focus on the practical, and often that's what we need. However, our collective history is interesting and informative. By understanding the research and sometimes heated debate, our thinking about what we do gains depth. We understand that this academic-seeming recapitulation may not appeal to all readers, but we also hope that you'll look through the papers we've referenced, and that this'll whet your appetite for more reading.

For additional reading, a good place to start is Rich Hickey's Clojure Bookshelf.[14]

---

13. http://dl.acm.org/citation.cfm?id=356842.356846
14. http://www.amazon.com/Clojure-Bookshelf/lm/R3LG3ZBZS4GCTH

Thinking in Clojure

When you choose to adopt Clojure (and its learning curve), you're selecting an implementation, a platform, and a set of features. You're also accepting certain limitations, some cultural baggage, and a peer group. Most important, you're learning to think in Clojure. This can be especially challenging if you're coming from an object-oriented language.

A clear understanding of the foundations of Clojure's design will help align your thinking with Clojure's implementation (see *Roots*). If you keep these guidelines in mind, you'll find yourself swimming with the current, rather than against it:

- Make reasoned choices
- Be reasonable
- Build just enough
- Compose
- Be precise
- Use what works

An explanation of each guideline follows.

Make Reasoned Choices

Clojure was developed using *reasoned choices*. Every decision that went into its features had trade-offs that were carefully weighed after time was taken to fully understand the consequences.

For example, compare Clojure's state-management facilities to the message-based protocol you find in Erlang. Clojure focuses on concurrent processes implemented on one host, whereas Erlang focuses on distributed systems. Clojure's atoms, refs, agents, and core.async library are a more efficient fit for that concurrency model than message-passing. This decision yields simple, robust concurrency at the cost of nearly transparent distributability. Horizontal scaling is more difficult, vertical scaling more effective.

Adopting this approach in your practice will help you find a clear path through your application's development. You'll be surprised less often, have sound arguments for your design decisions, and spend less time reworking implementations born of faulty assumptions.

To do that, we must first have the material to reason about. First we get to the heart of the problem domain and then we follow up with reasoning about what we've learned. These are the two keys to making reasoned choices: have material to reason about, and take the time to reason. *Think first, then do.* Hammock time is time worth taking.[1]

Be Reasonable

If you're reasoning about the problem, you should write software about which you and other developers can reason. You've probably encountered a code base that's full to the brim with mystery and surprise. Characteristics of reasonable code include clearly expressed intent, limited side effects, neatly separated concerns, and unambiguous naming. When you write your code this way, it's easier to comprehend the code base—you don't spend any time confused about what's happening. Reasonable code also tends to be simple.

Keep It Simple

Each concern in the structure of the Clojure programming language remains as distinct as possible. The implementation of persistent collections has nothing to do with futures; futures and channels are distinct, even though they both deal with asynchronous activities. As when a French chef practices *mise en place*, all of the ingredients are kept separate, to be combined only when the recipe requires it.

Keeping it simple means making sure that each concept avoids entangling itself with other concepts. Doing this in your practice means that each concept can be reasoned about, tested, and implemented without any incidental complexity. Entities are simplest when distinct and composable. Domain functions avoid complexity by avoiding side effects and concerning themselves only with entities in their domain.

---

1. https://www.youtube.com/watch?v=f84n5oFoZBc

Build Just Enough

Clojure has a sparse syntax and limited set of core features, a principle we might express as *build just enough*. Building just enough will help you, as an application developer, keep complexity at bay and avoid overengineering.

In every application, you're building a domain language. It's challenging, but by starting and staying small, you'll find yourself able to extend the language *using the language*. Guy Steele demonstrated these challenges at the 1998 ACM OOPSLA conference in a talk titled "Growing a Language."[2]

By building just enough, you're not weighed down with speculative functions and maybe-useful-eventually data. This helps you stay nimble when you need to make changes. As a bonus, it's easier to maintain a complete understanding of interconnections when you're assembling the application.

Compose

Following the path of simplicity and minimal implementation, you'll naturally end up with distinct, logically independent pieces. If those components are designed to compose cleanly and directly, you can avoid messy, integrated bridge code. Clojure developers tend to value *composability* for this reason.

Until this becomes second nature, evaluate your code for composability by using it from another component. If you find yourself wading through layer upon layer of wrappers and adapters, you'll know you fell off the wagon. The result will be a set of tidy interfaces to distinct, independent subsystems with clear communication channels. When a component is self-contained with a stable interface, it can grow easily and adapt quickly.

Be Precise

Clojure has an interesting lingo. The words that are used to talk about Clojure and have found their way into the language are precisely chosen. If you've watched "Simple Made Easy" from Strange Loop 2011,[3] then you're aware of Rich Hickey's love of language precision.

The lingo around Clojure reflects that precision. In cases where an original meaning has been drifted from in common parlance, there may be some ambiguity of meaning (for example, *simple*). In other cases a disused word

---

2. https://www.youtube.com/watch?v=_ahvzDzKdB0
3. http://www.infoq.com/presentations/Simple-Made-Easy

has been given a place of prominence (*reify*, *elide*). Finally, some words have been created out of thin air (for example, *seqable*).

Hidden under the Clojure dictionary is another principle to bear in mind: *be precise*. When each entity, function, and query at the core of your application is both precise and concise, you can avoid ambiguity and communicate clearly with other developers and your future self. Entities typify one concept. Functions effect a single transformation. Queries ask simple questions and return unambiguous results. Other developers and your future self will be able to reason more effectively about your code.

Use What Works

Clojure has been assembled out of established ideas. That exemplifies one of its core principles: *use what works*. Our desire to invent and deadline pressures can make a thorough evaluation of an existing system hard to justify, so we sometimes find ourselves re-solving solved problems.

When building an application, you wouldn't write an authentication and authorization system from scratch, a web framework, and certainly not a database—not if you could use an existing tool that solves the problem. This is as true of ideas as it is of libraries.

When encountering a problem, a savvy developer will spend some time trying to find a sound existing solution. It's possible to find a library in Clojure, but equally possible is the discovery of an implementation in another language that can be adapted, or in some cases a paper on the subject that lacks a strong implementation. By adopting a proven solution, you gain stability and confidence, and usually save time in the bargain. You can also draw on the experiences and advice of others currently using the solution.

Wrapping Up

Now you're conversant in the most important principles of developing Clojure applications in the large. Adopting, or at least being aware of, these guidelines will help you think like a Clojure developer when building software. This list isn't comprehensive, but it covers the biggest of the bullet points. Of course, you have your own playbook and should mix in the things you find valuable.

Bibliography

[BG81]   Philip A. Bernstein and Nathan Goodman. Concurrency Control in Distributed Database Systems. *ACM Computing Surveys (CSUR)*. 13[2]:185-221, 1981, June.

[Chu36]   Alonzo Church. An Unsolvable Problem of Elementary Number Theory. *American Journal of Mathematics*. 58[2], 1936, April.

[DSST89]   James R. Driscoll, Neil Sarnak, Daniel D. Sleator, and Robert E. Tarjan. Making Data Structures Persistent. *Journal of Computer and System Sciences*. 38[1], 1989, February.

[Fow03]   Martin Fowler. *Patterns of Enterprise Application Architecture*. Addison-Wesley Longman, Reading, MA, 2003.

[FW76]   Daniel Friedman and David Wise. The Impact of Applicative Programming on Multiprocessing. *International Conference on Parallel Processing*. 263-272, 1976.

[HB12]   Stuart Halloway and Aaron Bedra. *Programming Clojure (2nd edition)*. The Pragmatic Bookshelf, Raleigh, NC, and Dallas, TX, 2nd, 2012.

[HB77]   Carl Hewitt and Henry C. Baker Jr.. The Incremental Garbage Collection of Processes. *Proceedings of the 1977 symposium on Artificial Intelligence and Programming Languages*. 55-59, 1977.

[HM76]   Peter Henderson and James H. Morris Jr.. An Unsolvable Problem of Elementary Number Theory. *Proceeding POPL '76 Proceedings of the 3rd ACM SIGACT-SIGPLAN symposium on Principles on Programming Languages*. 95-103, 1976, January.

[Hoa78]   C. A. R. Hoare. Communicating Sequential Processes. *Communications of the ACM*. 21[8]:666-677, 1978, August.

[McC60]   John McCarthy. Recursive Functions of Symbolic Expressions and Their Computation by Machine, Part I. *Communications of the ACM.* 1960, April.

[McI60]   M. Douglas McIlroy. Macro Instruction Extensions of Compiler Languages. *Communications of the ACM.* 1960, April.

[Ree78]   David Patrick Reed. *Naming and Synchronization in a Decentralized Computer System.* MIT Press, Cambridge, MA, 1978.

[Vui73]   Jean Vuillemin. Correct and Optimal Implementations of Recursion in a Simple Programming Language. *STOC '73: Proceedings of the fifth annual ACM Symposium on Theory of Computing.* 224-239, 1973.

[Wad71]   Christopher Wadsworth. *Semantics and Pragmatics of the Lambda-calculus.* Oxford University Press, New York, NY, 1971.

Index

Clojure and Macros

Get up to speed on all that Clojure has to offer, and fine-tune your understanding and use of macros.

Programming Clojure (2nd edition)

If you want to keep up with the significant changes in this important language, you need the second edition of *Programming Clojure*. Stu and Aaron describe the modifications to the numerics system in Clojure 1.3, explain new Clojure concepts such as Protocols and Datatypes, and teach you how to think in Clojure.

Stuart Halloway and Aaron Bedra
(296 pages) ISBN: 9781934356869. $35
https://pragprog.com/book/shcloj2

Mastering Clojure Macros

Level up your skills by taking advantage of Clojure's powerful macro system. Macros make hard things possible and normal things easy. They can be tricky to use, and this book will help you deftly navigate the terrain. You'll discover how to write straightforward code that avoids duplication and clarifies your intentions. You'll learn how and why to write macros. You'll learn to recognize situations when using a macro would (and wouldn't!) be helpful. And you'll use macros to remove unnecessary code and build new language features.

Colin Jones
(120 pages) ISBN: 9781941222225. $17
https://pragprog.com/book/cjclojure

Even More Clojure

With Clojure for the web, and useful patterns in both Clojure and Scala.

Web Development with Clojure

If the usual patchwork of web development tools and languages just isn't cutting it for you, you need *Web Development With Clojure*. Clojure gives you the rich infrastructure of the JVM with the expressive power of a modern functional language. It combines excellent performance with rapid development—and you can exploit these virtues for web app development. With step-by-step examples, you'll learn how to harness that power and richness to build modern web applications.

Download the author's free guide to Clojure Clojure Distilled

Dmitri Sotnikov
(232 pages) ISBN: 9781937785642. $36
https://pragprog.com/book/dswdcloj

Functional Programming Patterns in Scala and Clojure

Solve real-life programming problems with a fraction of the code that pure object-oriented programming requires. Use Scala and Clojure to solve in-depth problems and see how familiar object-oriented patterns can become more concise with functional programming and patterns. Your code will be more declarative, with fewer bugs and lower maintenance costs.

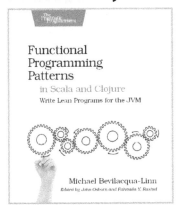

Michael Bevilacqua-Linn
(256 pages) ISBN: 9781937785475. $36
https://pragprog.com/book/mbfpp

The Joy of Math and Healthy Programming

Rediscover the joy and fascinating weirdness of pure mathematics, and learn how to take a healthier approach to programming.

Good Math

Mathematics is beautiful—and it can be fun and exciting as well as practical. *Good Math* is your guide to some of the most intriguing topics from two thousand years of mathematics: from Egyptian fractions to Turing machines; from the real meaning of numbers to proof trees, group symmetry, and mechanical computation. If you've ever wondered what lay beyond the proofs you struggled to complete in high school geometry, or what limits the capabilities of the computer on your desk, this is the book for you.

Mark C. Chu-Carroll
(282 pages) ISBN: 9781937785338. $34
https://pragprog.com/book/mcmath

The Healthy Programmer

To keep doing what you love, you need to maintain your own systems, not just the ones you write code for. Regular exercise and proper nutrition help you learn, remember, concentrate, and be creative—skills critical to doing your job well. Learn how to change your work habits, master exercises that make working at a computer more comfortable, and develop a plan to keep fit, healthy, and sharp for years to come.

This book is intended only as an informative guide for those wishing to know more about health issues. In no way is this book intended to replace, countermand, or conflict with the advice given to you by your own healthcare provider including Physician, Nurse Practitioner, Physician Assistant, Registered Dietician, and other licensed professionals.

Joe Kutner
(254 pages) ISBN: 9781937785314. $36
https://pragprog.com/book/jkthp

Seven in Seven

From Web Frameworks to Concurrency Models, see what the rest of the world is doing with this introduction to seven different approaches.

Seven Web Frameworks in Seven Weeks

Whether you need a new tool or just inspiration, *Seven Web Frameworks in Seven Weeks* explores modern options, giving you a taste of each with ideas that will help you create better apps. You'll see frameworks that leverage modern programming languages, employ unique architectures, live client-side instead of server-side, or embrace type systems. You'll see everything from familiar Ruby and JavaScript to the more exotic Erlang, Haskell, and Clojure.

Jack Moffitt, Fred Daoud
(302 pages) ISBN: 9781937785635. $38
https://pragprog.com/book/7web

Seven Concurrency Models in Seven Weeks

Your software needs to leverage multiple cores, handle thousands of users and terabytes of data, and continue working in the face of both hardware and software failure. Concurrency and parallelism are the keys, and *Seven Concurrency Models in Seven Weeks* equips you for this new world. See how emerging technologies such as actors and functional programming address issues with traditional threads and locks development. Learn how to exploit the parallelism in your computer's GPU and leverage clusters of machines with MapReduce and Stream Processing. And do it all with the confidence that comes from using tools that help you write crystal clear, high-quality code.

Paul Butcher
(206 pages) ISBN: 9781937785659. $38
https://pragprog.com/book/pb7con

The Pragmatic Bookshelf

The Pragmatic Bookshelf features books written by developers for developers. The titles continue the well-known Pragmatic Programmer style and continue to garner awards and rave reviews. As development gets more and more difficult, the Pragmatic Programmers will be there with more titles and products to help you stay on top of your game.

Visit Us Online

This Book's Home Page
https://pragprog.com/book/vmclojeco
Source code from this book, errata, and other resources. Come give us feedback, too!

Register for Updates
https://pragprog.com/updates
Be notified when updates and new books become available.

Join the Community
https://pragprog.com/community
Read our weblogs, join our online discussions, participate in our mailing list, interact with our wiki, and benefit from the experience of other Pragmatic Programmers.

New and Noteworthy
https://pragprog.com/news
Check out the latest pragmatic developments, new titles and other offerings.

Save on the eBook

Save on the eBook versions of this title. Owning the paper version of this book entitles you to purchase the electronic versions at a terrific discount.

PDFs are great for carrying around on your laptop—they are hyperlinked, have color, and are fully searchable. Most titles are also available for the iPhone and iPod touch, Amazon Kindle, and other popular e-book readers.

Buy now at *https://pragprog.com/coupon*

Contact Us

Online Orders:	*https://pragprog.com/catalog*
Customer Service:	*support@pragprog.com*
International Rights:	*translations@pragprog.com*
Academic Use:	*academic@pragprog.com*
Write for Us:	*http://write-for-us.pragprog.com*
Or Call:	+1 800-699-7764

Milton Keynes UK
Ingram Content Group UK Ltd.
UKHW031055061024
449279UK00007B/165